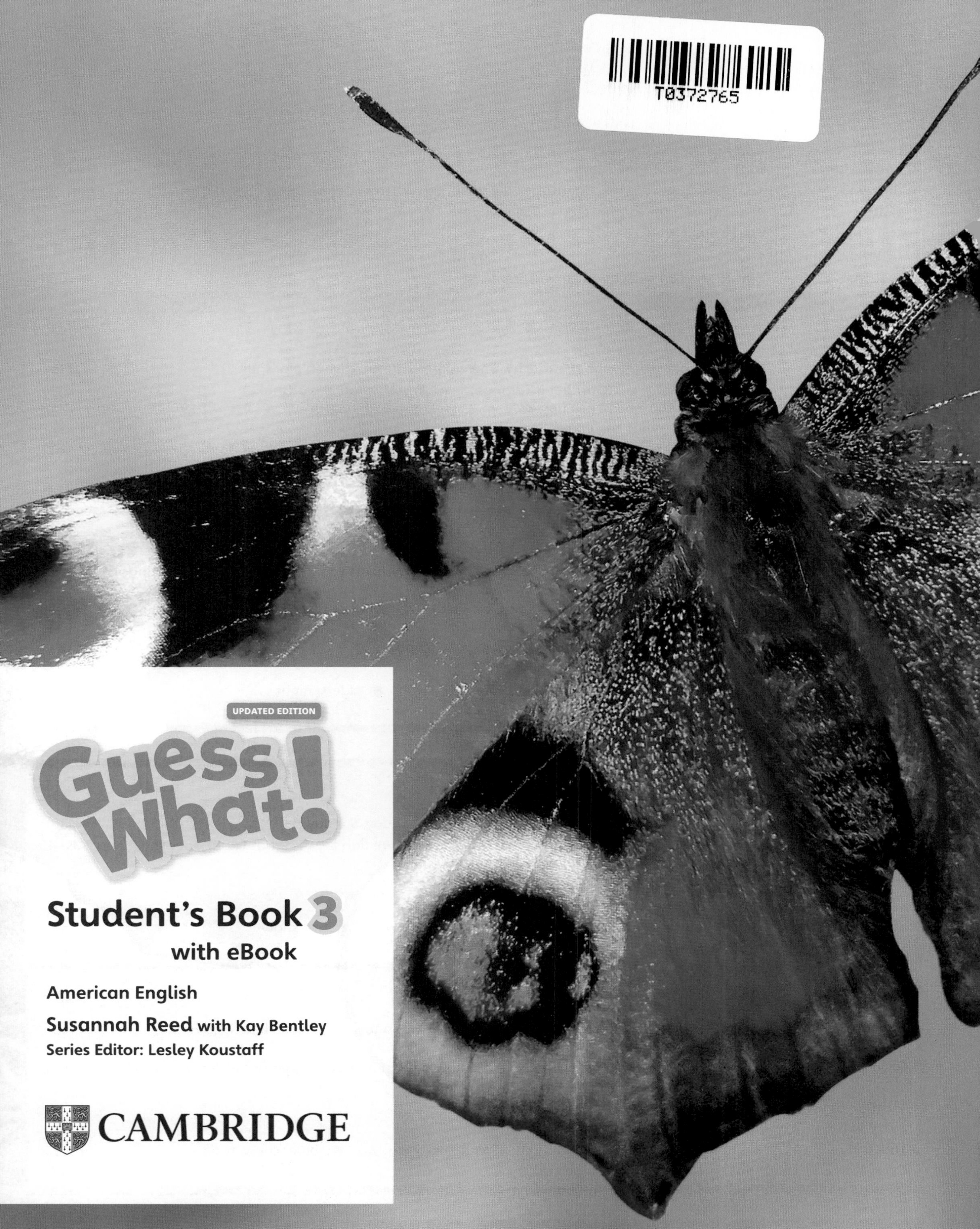
T0372765
UPDATED EDITION
Guess What!
Student's Book 3
with eBook
American English
Susannah Reed with Kay Bentley
Series Editor: Lesley Koustaff
CAMBRIDGE

Contents

Welcome

Guess What!

1 Listen and point.

2 Listen, point, and repeat.

3 Listen and say the names.

4 Think Describe and guess who.

She's four years old.

Anna!

1 Lucas
2 Max
3 Lily
4 Tom
5 Anna

→ Workbook page 4

Questions, questions,
I like asking questions.
What's your name?
How old are you?
What's your favorite color?

Questions, questions,
I like asking questions.
Do you like sports?
Do you have a pet?
Can you draw a picture of me?

Questions, questions,
I like asking questions.

6 Match the questions to the answers.

1. What's your name?
2. How old are you?
3. What's your favorite color?
4. Do you like sports?
5. Do you have a pet?
6. Can you draw a picture of me?

a Yes, I do. I have a dog.

b I'm ten years old.

c Yes, I do. My favorite sports are swimming and tennis.

d Yes, I can. I like art.

e My name's Lily.

f My favorite color is yellow.

7 About Me Ask and answer with a friend.

My favorite color is blue.

8 Listen and repeat.

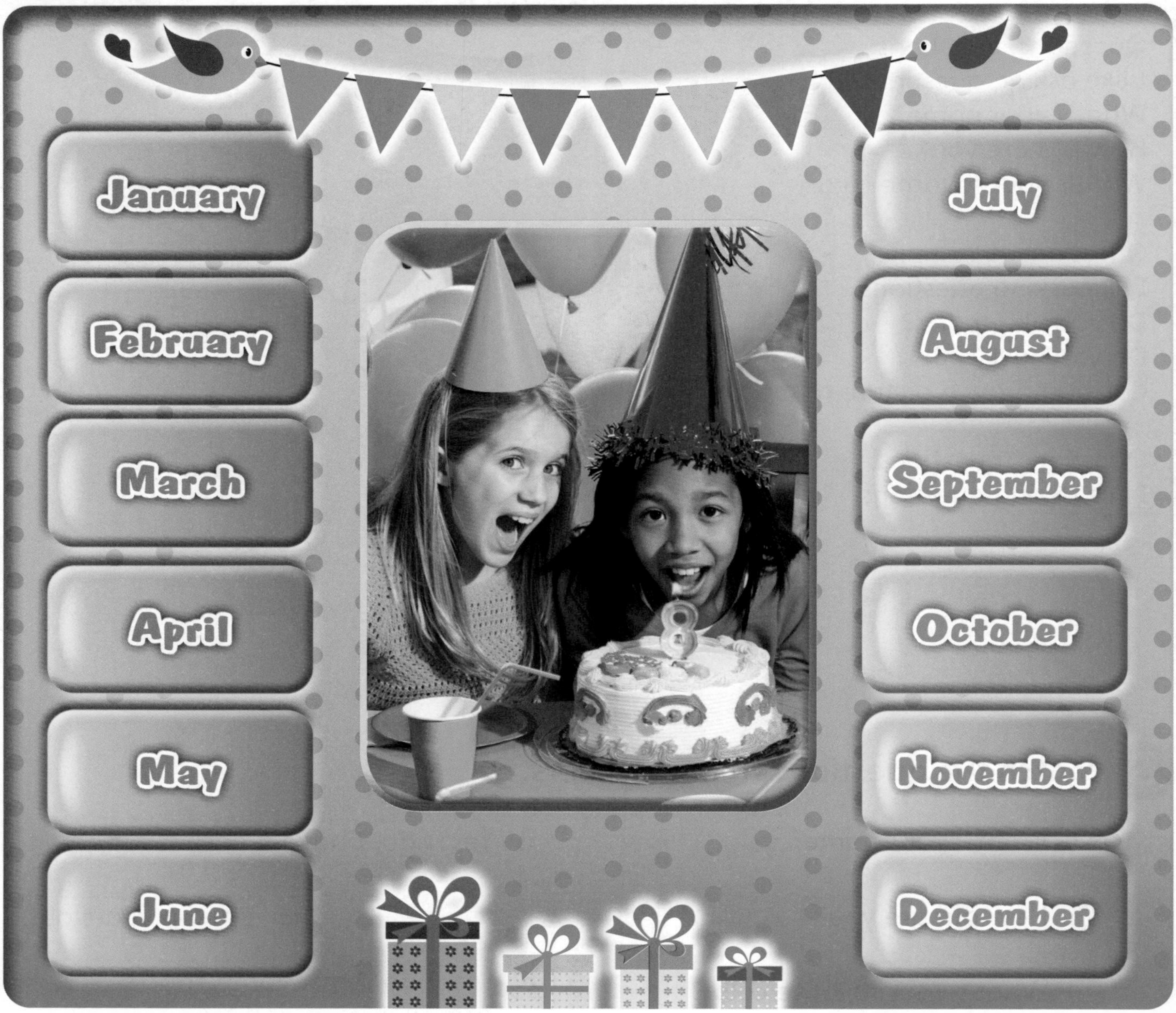
January
February
March
April
May
June
July
August
September
October
November
December

9 Listen and say the next month.

January, February, March …

April!

10 Ask and answer with a friend.

When's your birthday?

It's in June.

Remember

When's your birthday?
It's in December.

11 Go to page 102. Listen and repeat the chant.

Grammar fun!

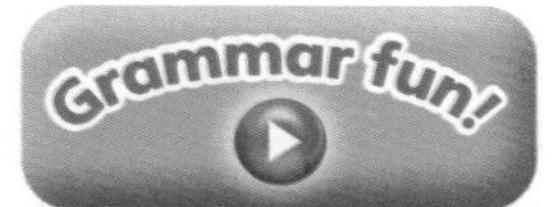

→ Workbook page 6

Skills: *Reading and speaking*

Let's start! Do you have an email pen pal?

12 0.08 Read and listen.

Hi. My name's Juan. I'm ten years old. My birthday is in March.

I live in a small house with my family. I have two sisters and a brother. I don't have any pets, but I like animals.

I like basketball and field hockey, but my favorite sport is baseball. I like fishing, too.

What about you?

Email me back.

Juan

13 Read again and answer the questions.

1 How old is Juan?
2 When's his birthday?
3 How many brothers does he have?
4 Does he like animals?
5 Does he like sports?

14 About Me Ask and answer with a friend.

How old are you?
Do you have any brothers or sisters?
Do you have a pet?
What's your favorite sport?

Writing

Workbook page 7: Write an email to a pen pal.

15
0.09
Story
Read and listen. Watch.
1
Happy birthday, Lily!
Thanks, Tom! Thanks everyone for your presents!
2
What's this present?
I don't kno
Open it, Lily!
3
It's a cell phone!
And look at this!
4
Treasure Hunt.
Find 7 things in 7 days.
Text 123 to join.
A surprise at the end!
5
Let's do the treasure hunt together!
Good idea.
6
Dad, can we do this treasure hunt, please?
Yes, of course! It sounds fun.
123 – there!
10
Value: Work together
→ Workbook page 8

16 Listen and repeat. Then act.

fly this kite | do this treasure hunt | go to the movie theater | play outside | go to the sports center

Say it!

17 Listen and repeat.

Snakes make trails with their tails.

→ Workbook page 9

What can you see in a landscape painting?

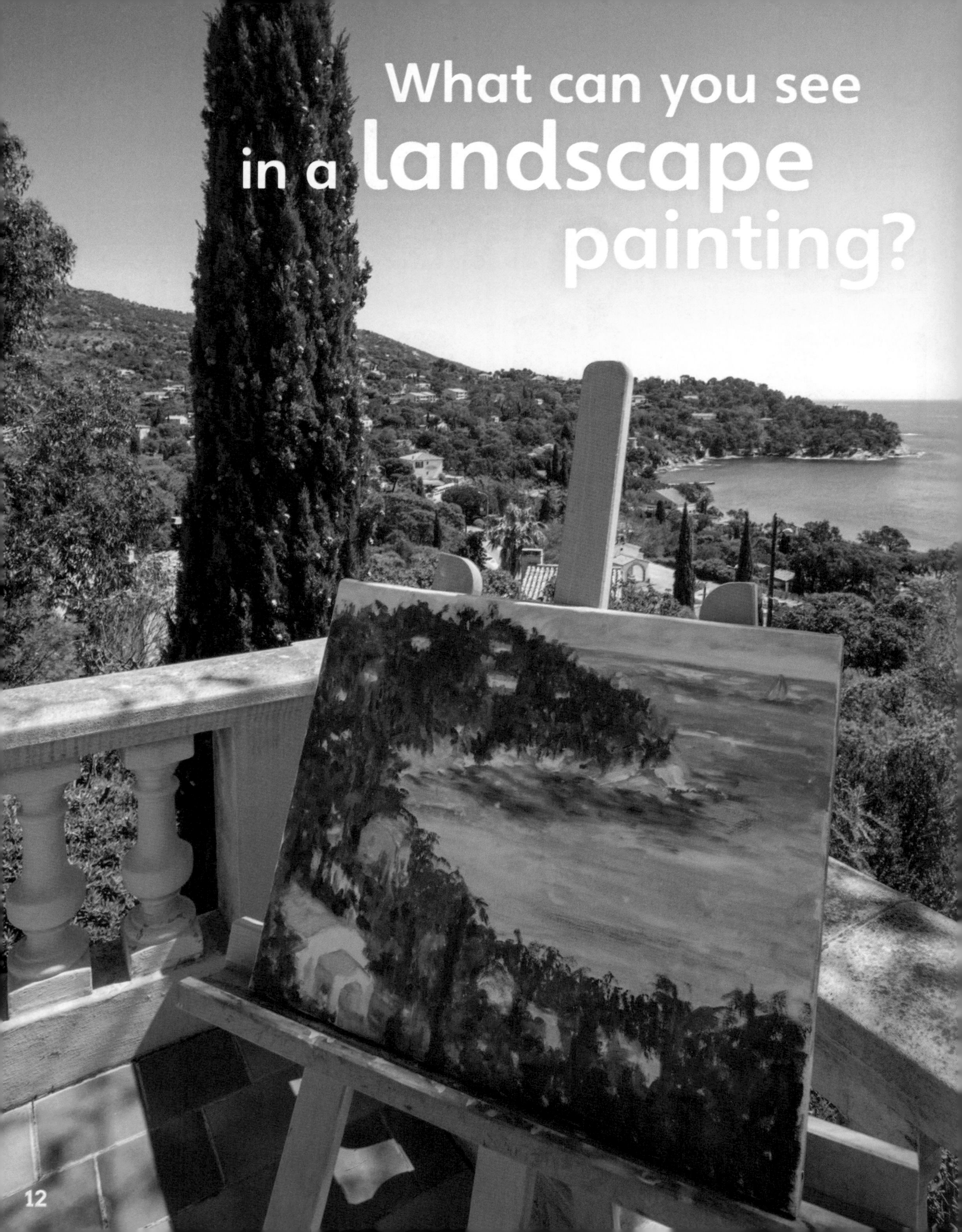

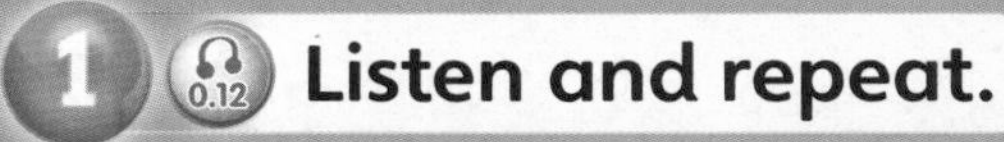

1 0.12 Listen and repeat.

river ocean waterfall forest mountain

2 CLIL Watch the video.

3 What can you see in the landscape paintings?

Let's collaborate!

4 What would you like to paint in a landscape painting?

→ Workbook page 10

1 In the yard

Guess What!

1 Listen and point. (1.01)

2 Listen, point, and repeat. (1.02)

1. tree
2. leaf
3. caterpillar
4. rabbit
5. butterfly
6. flower
7. grass
8. turtle
9. guinea pig
10. snail

3 Listen and say the words. (1.03)

4 Think Describe and guess what.

It's a plant. It's green.

Grass!

→ Workbook page 12

5 Sing the song.

My pet is white.
Your pet is gray.
Our pets aren't big,
They're small.
Where are our pets?
Can you see our pets?

Her pet is white.
His pet is gray.
Their pets aren't big,
They're small.
Where are their pets?
Can you see their pets?

6 Read and match. Then say the animal.

1

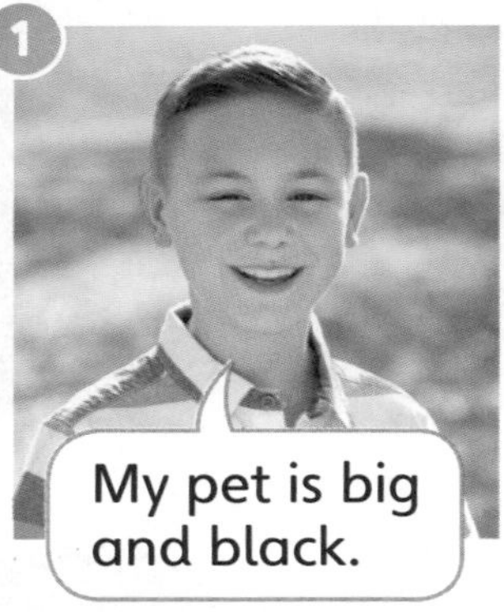

My pet is big and black.

2

Her pet is small and orange.

3

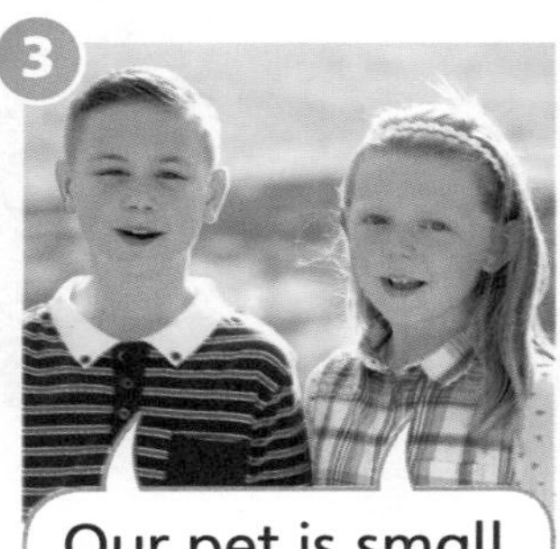

Our pet is small and yellow.

4

Their pet is gray and beautiful.

a

b

c

d

7 Look at the photographs. Ask and answer with a friend.

Number 3. Is their pet a bird?

Yes, it is.

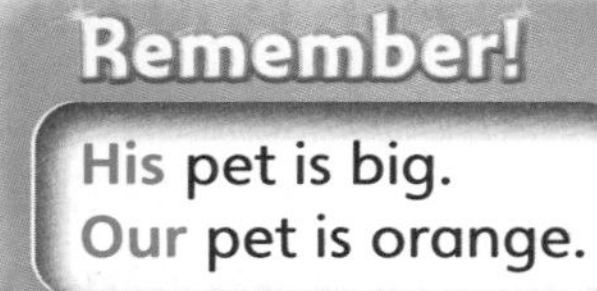

Remember!

His pet is big.
Our pet is orange.

8 Listen and repeat.

9 1.06 Listen and say the numbers.

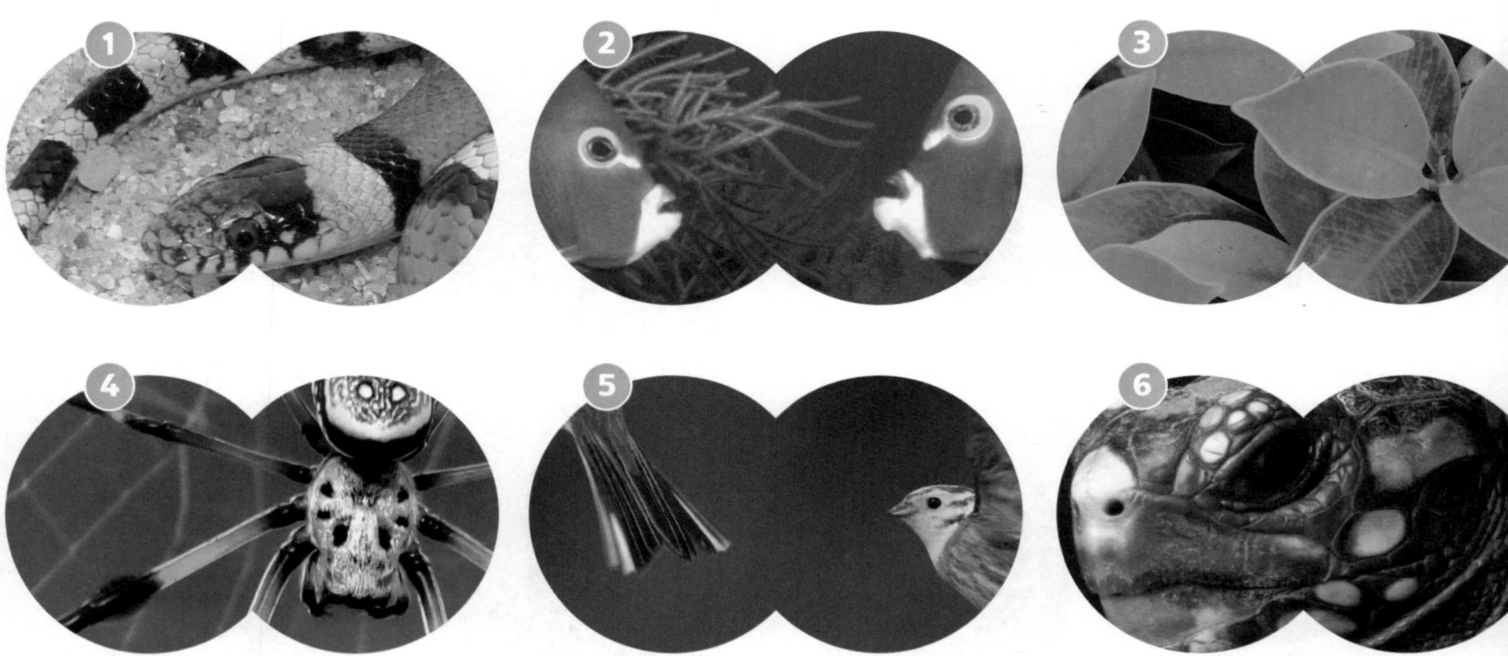

10 Look at the photographs.
Ask and answer with a friend.

11 1.07 Go to page 102. Listen and repeat the chant.

Remember!

What's that?
It's a snake.
What are those?
They're leaves.

→ Workbook page 14

Skills: *Listening and speaking*

Let's start! **What can you see at the zoo?**

12 Listen and match.

House of bugs

a

b

c

d

13 Listen again and say *true* or *false*.

1 Lucy likes snails.
2 Ryan likes ants.
3 Sara doesn't like the butterfly.
4 Jake doesn't like caterpillars.

14 Ask and answer with a friend.

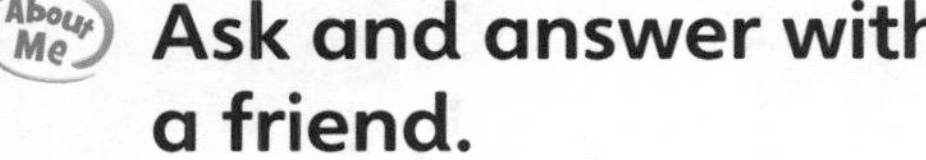

What is your favorite bug?
What color is it?
What bugs can you see outside?

Writing

Workbook page 15: Write about your favorite bug.

15 1.10 Story Read and listen. Watch.

1
Max loves soccer.
What's that?
It's a message!

2
Find a toy tiger.

3
A toy tiger? Where
Can I help?
Not now, Anna.

4
Look! Behind that tree! What's that?
Are those ears and a tail?
Yes! Come on!

5
Oh! It's a cat!
I can help ...
Not now, Anna

6
Wait! Is this your tiger, Anna?
Yes, it is.
Can we borrow it, please?

7
Yes, you can! Here you are.
Thank you, Anna.
Sorry, Anna. Thank you.

 Value: Respect and listen to others

→ Workbook page 16

  Talk Time **Listen and repeat. Then act.**

computer game | toy car | eraser | camera | book

Say it!

17 1.12 **Listen and repeat.**

Chimpanzees eat and sleep in trees.

→ Workbook page 17

What types of habitats are there?

1 Listen and repeat. 1.13

1 desert

2 rain forest

3 grassland

4 tundra

2 CLIL Watch the video.

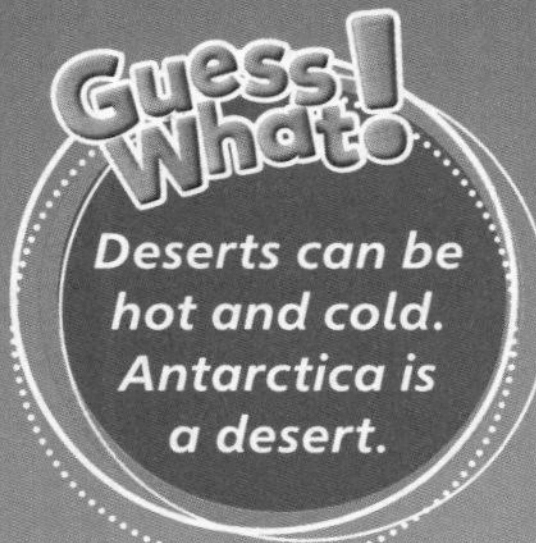

3 Match the habitats with the groups of animals.

1. monkey, crocodile, snake
2. lion, giraffe, snake

desert
grassland
rainforest
tundra

3. spider, snake, camel
4. goat, sheep, bear

4 What type of habitat would you like to visit?

Let's collaborate!

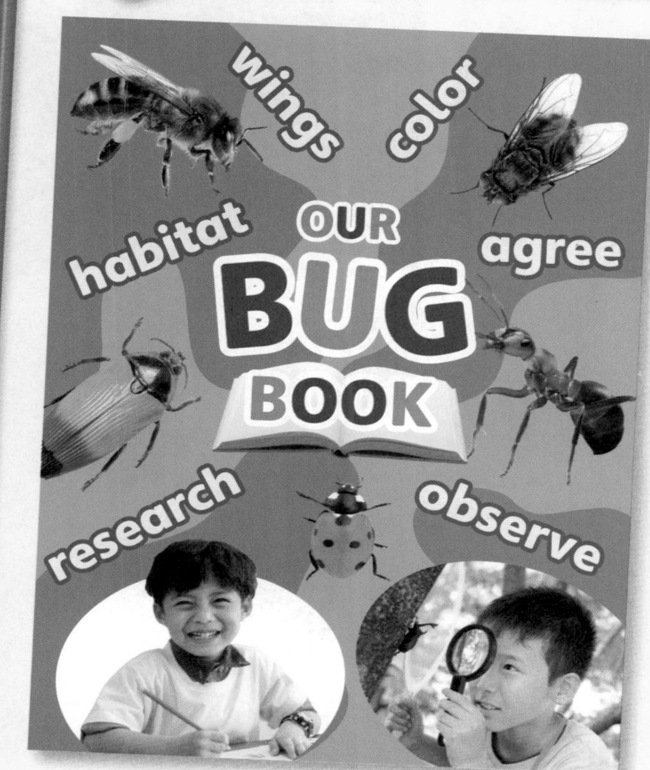

→ Workbook page 18

2 At school

Look!

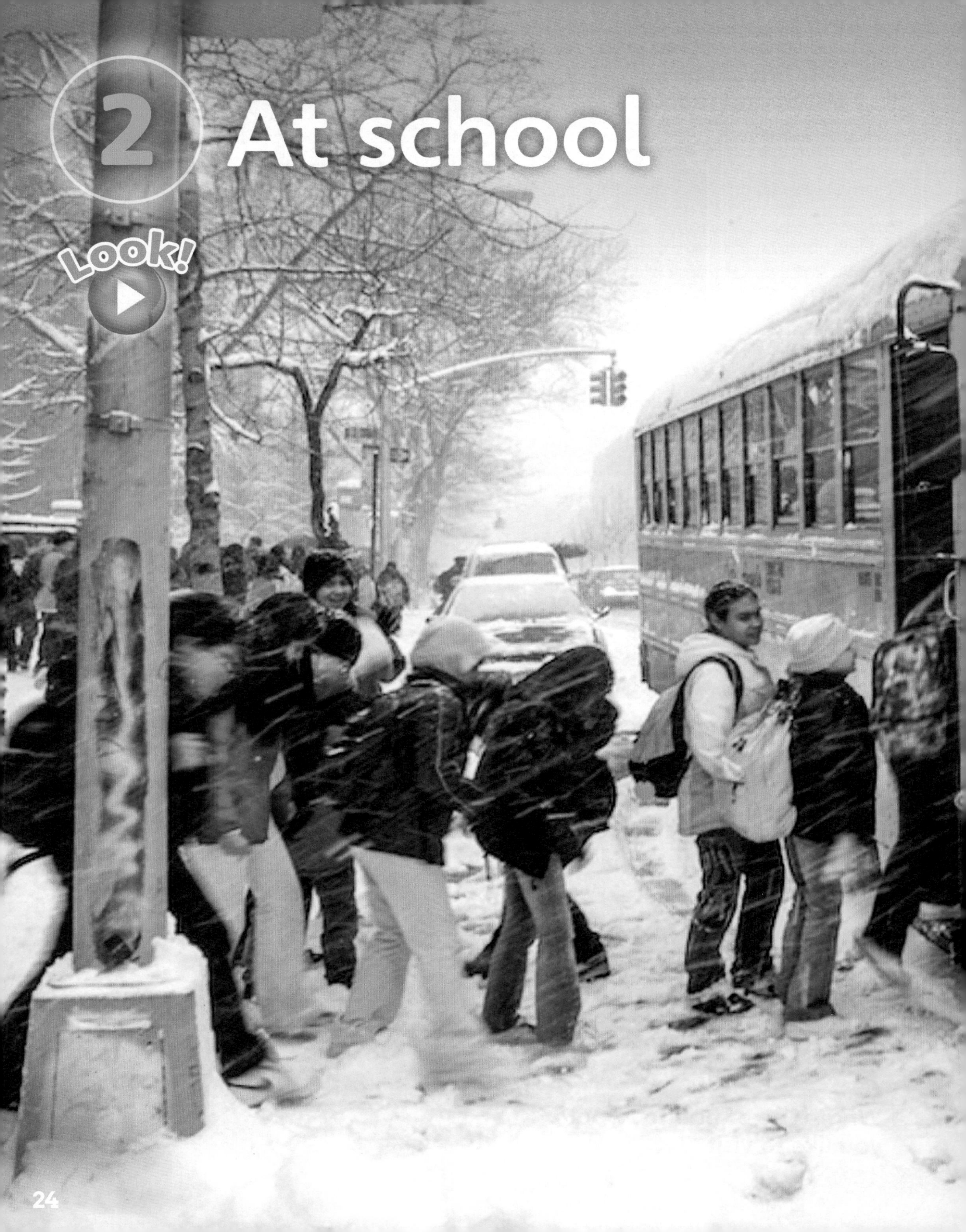

SCHOOL BUS
117
Guess What!

1 🎧 2.01 **Listen and point.**

2 🎧 2.02 **Listen, point, and repeat.**

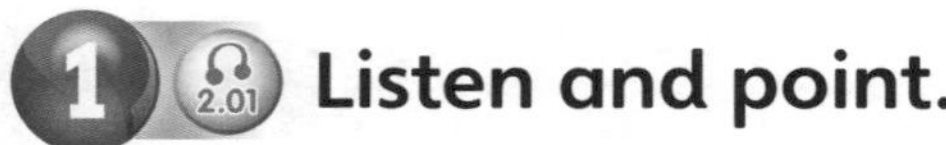

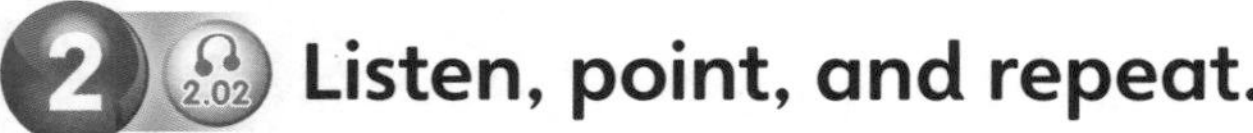

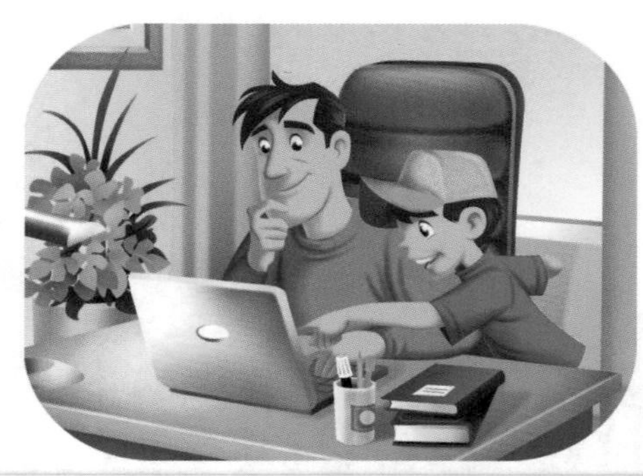

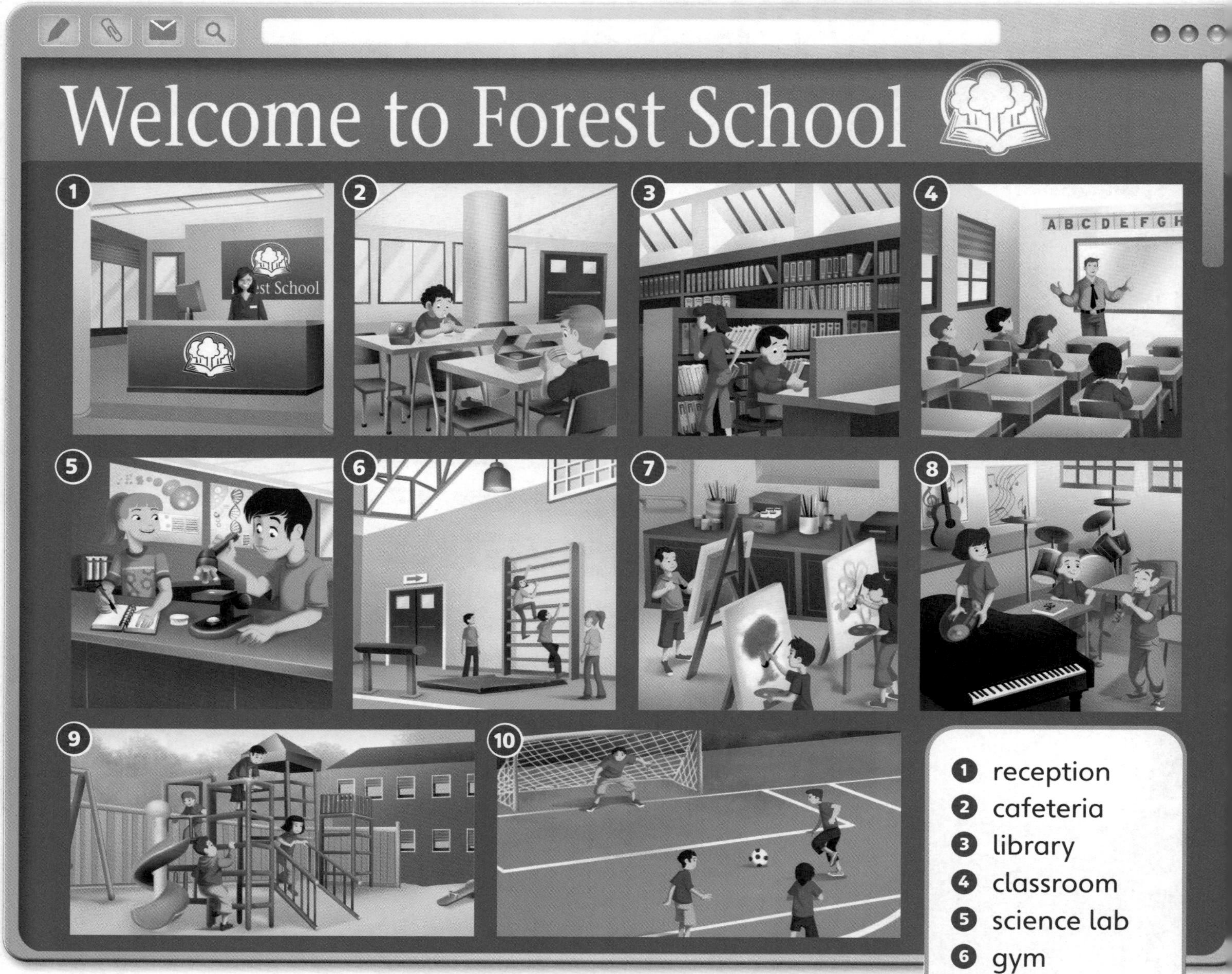
Welcome to Forest School
1
2
3
4
A B C D E F G H
5
6
7
8
9
10

1. reception
2. cafeteria
3. library
4. classroom
5. science lab
6. gym
7. art room
8. music room
9. playground
10. sports field

3 🎧 2.03 **Listen and say the places.**

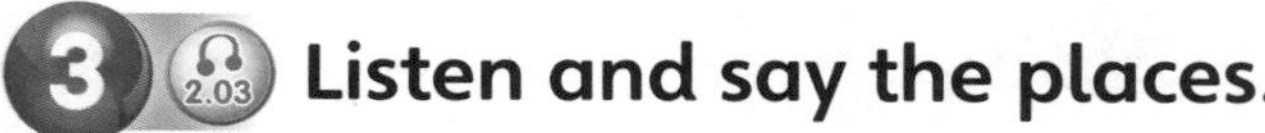

4 Think **Describe and guess where.**

This is Lily's favorite room.

Music room!

→ Workbook page 20

Dave and Daisy, where are you?
We're in the cafeteria.
Where are Dave and Daisy?
They're in the cafeteria.

Max and Mary, where are you?
We're in the music room.
Where are Max and Mary?
They're in the music room.

Sam and Susie, where are you?
We're on the sports field.
Where are Sam and Susie?
They're on the sports field.

6 Read and match.

1 

2 

3 

a We're in the art room.

b We're on the playground.

c We're in the library.

7 Look at the pictures in activities 5 and 6. Ask and answer with a friend.

Where are they?

They're on the playground.

Where are they?
They're **on the sports field.**

8 2.05 Listen and repeat.

1

2

9 2.06 Look and find. Then listen and say the numbers.

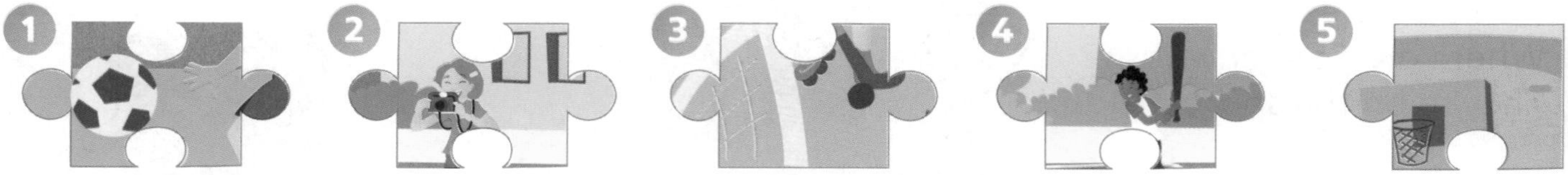

1 2 3 4 5

a b c d e

10 Look at the picture. Ask and answer with a friend.

What are they doing?

They're playing baseball.

11 2.07 Go to page 102. Listen and repeat the chant.

Remember

What **are** you doing?
We**'re** playing baseball.

Skills: *Reading and speaking*

What places can you find in your school?

12 Read and listen. Then match.

2.08

1 My name's Lisa. Can you find a photograph of me? I'm standing outside my school. My school is big.

2 This is the playground. It's a big playground. Some children are playing a game of basketball. I like basketball, but my favorite sport is tennis.

3 This is a classroom. There's a board and some desks and chairs. These children are doing math. I like math, but my favorite class is art. I like drawing and painting.

4 This is my favorite room. It's our school library. There are lots of books, and I like reading. There are a lot of children in the library today.

a

b

c

d

13 Read again and answer the questions.

1 Is Lisa's school big or small?
2 What is Lisa's favorite sport?
3 What are the children in the classroom doing?
4 Does Lisa like reading?

14 About Me Make sentences about your school. Say *true* or *false*.

Our school is small.

False. It's big.

Writing

Workbook page 23: Write a description of your school.

→ Workbook page 24

16 Listen and repeat. Then act.

pick up this litter | clean the living room | play nicely | put those toys in your room

Say it!

17 Listen and repeat.

Tigers sometimes fight at night.

→ Workbook page 25

What materials can we recycle?

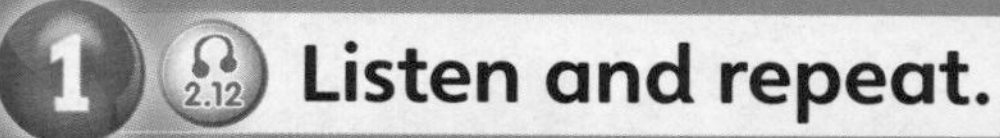

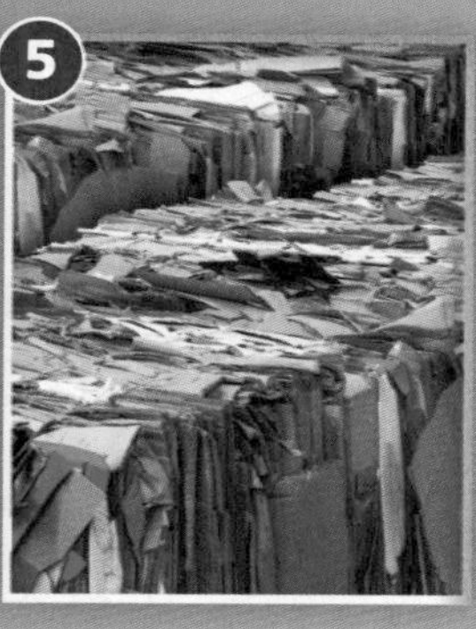

recycling bin | paper | can | bottle | cardboard

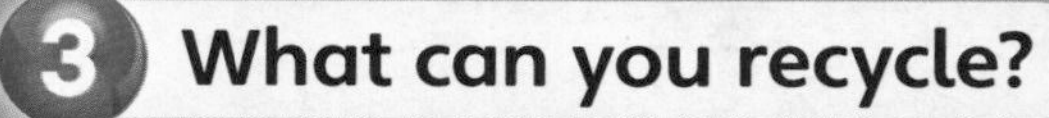

4 What materials does your school recycle?

Let's collaborate!

Review

Units 1 and 2

1 Find the months in the word puzzles.

2 2.13 Listen and match the months to the photographs.

3 Look at each photograph. Answer the questions.

1 Where are they?
2 What are they doing?

4 Make your own word puzzles for your friend.

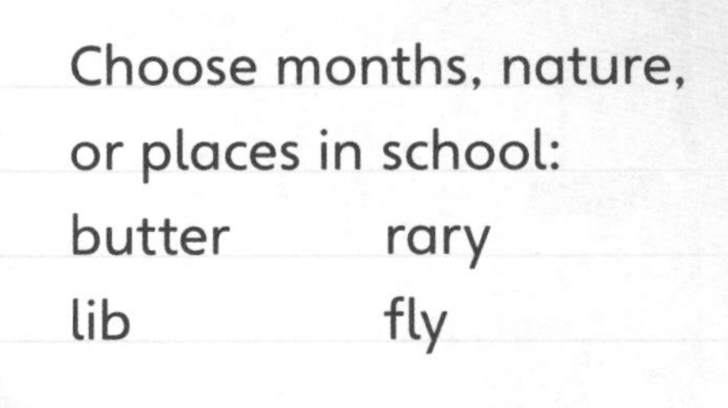

Carnival Day

Sports Day

Children's Day

Teacher's Day

→ Workbook pages 28–29

5 Play the game.

What's that?

It's a rabbit. Good. I have a rabbit.

What are those?

They're spiders. I don't have spiders.

3 School days

Guess What!

1 3.01 **Listen and point.**

2 3.02 **Listen, point, and repeat.**

1. Monday
2. Tuesday
3. Wednesday
4. Thursday
5. Friday
6. Saturday
7. Sunday

3 3.03 **Listen and say the days.**

4 Think **Make sentences and guess the days.**

He has math, and she has science.

Monday!

→ Workbook page 30

5 Sing the song.

We have math on Monday.
We don't have math on Tuesday.
Do we have math on Wednesday?
Yes, we do – on Wednesday, too.
We have math on Monday and Wednesday.

We have English on Thursday.
We don't have English on Friday.
Do we have English on Monday?
Yes, we do – on Monday, too.
We have English on Monday and Thursday.

6 Make a schedule with a friend. Ask and answer.

7 Make sentences about your schedule. Say *true* or *false*.

We have music on Monday and Friday.

False!

We don't have music on Wednesday.

True!

Remember!

Do we have science on Tuesday?
Yes, we do. No, we don't.

→ Workbook page 31

8 3.05 Listen and look. Then listen and repeat.

in the morning

lunchtime

in the afternoon

dinnertime

after school

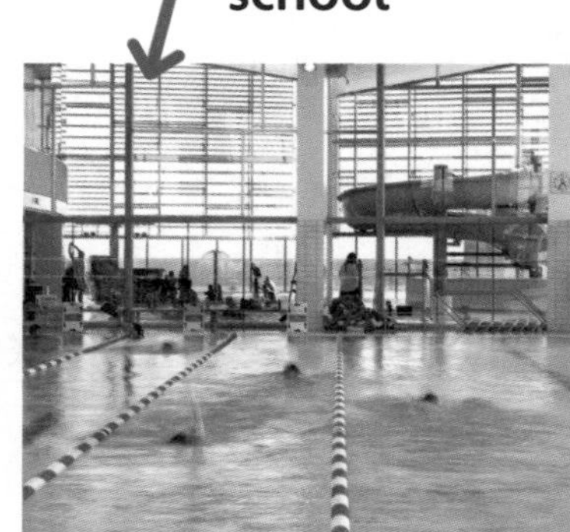

9 Now read and answer the questions.

1 What classes does Amy have in the morning?
2 What classes does Amy have in the afternoon?
3 What club does Amy have after school?
4 What class does Amy have before lunch?
5 What class does Amy have after lunch?

Amy has math and English in the morning.

10  Choose a day from your schedule. Play a guessing game.

What do you have in the morning?

I have math and science.

Is it Wednesday?

Yes, it is.

11 3.06 Go to page 102. Listen and repeat the chant.

Remember

What club **does she have** after school?
She has swimming club after school.

→ Workbook page 32

Skills: *Listening and speaking*

Do you have a favorite day of the week?

12 Listen and choose.

3.07

Favorite day: Sunday
Morning: Swimming competition
Afternoon: Art club
Evening: Movie theater trip

Favorite day: Friday
Morning: Math test
Afternoon: Field trip to a farm
Evening: Field hockey club

Favorite day: Saturday
Morning: Art competition
Afternoon: Movie theater trip
Evening: Dance club

13 Listen again and say *true* or *false*.

3.08

1 Caleb's favorite class is math.
2 Salima's favorite class is music.
3 Maddie likes playing field hockey.
4 Salima likes dancing.

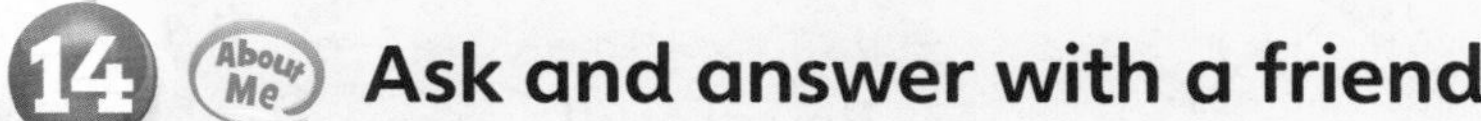

14 Ask and answer with a friend.

About Me

What's your favorite class?
What clubs do you have after school?
Do you like competitions?
Do you like school tests?

Writing

Workbook page 33: Write about your favorite day.

15 3.09 Story **Read and listen. Watch.**

1
Find this painting.

2
What day is today?
It's Saturday.
Great! I like art. Let's go to the art gallery.

3
Is the art gallery open on Saturdays?
Yes, it is.
Come on. Let's go!

4
OK. Here we are.
Now where's the painting?
Over there!

5
What can we do now?
We can't take a photograph of the painting.
I have an idea!

6
Be careful!
Are you OK, Tom?
Yes, I'm fine. Don't worry.

7
It's very good, Tom.
What do you think, Max?

 Value: Be resourceful

→ Workbook page 34

  Talk Time **Listen and repeat. Then act.**

art gallery | hospital | sports center | movie theater | library

1

2

Say it!

17 3.11 **Listen and repeat.**

Goats need warm coats in the snow.

→ Workbook page 35

Which animals are nocturnal?

1 Listen and repeat. 3.12

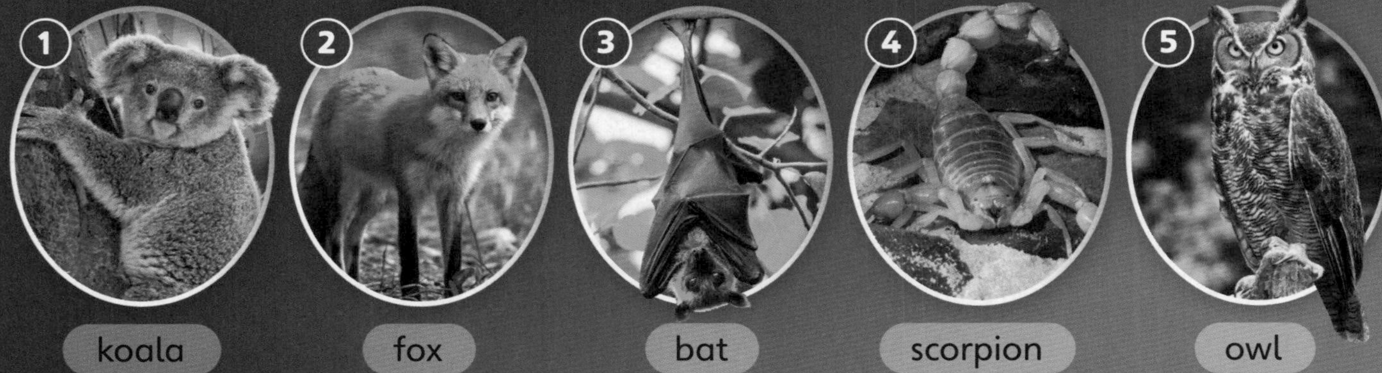

koala fox bat scorpion owl

2 CLIL Watch the video.

Guess What!
At night, owls can see mice 18 m in front of them.

3 Which animals are nocturnal?

Let's collaborate!

4 Which animals in your country are nocturnal?

4 My day

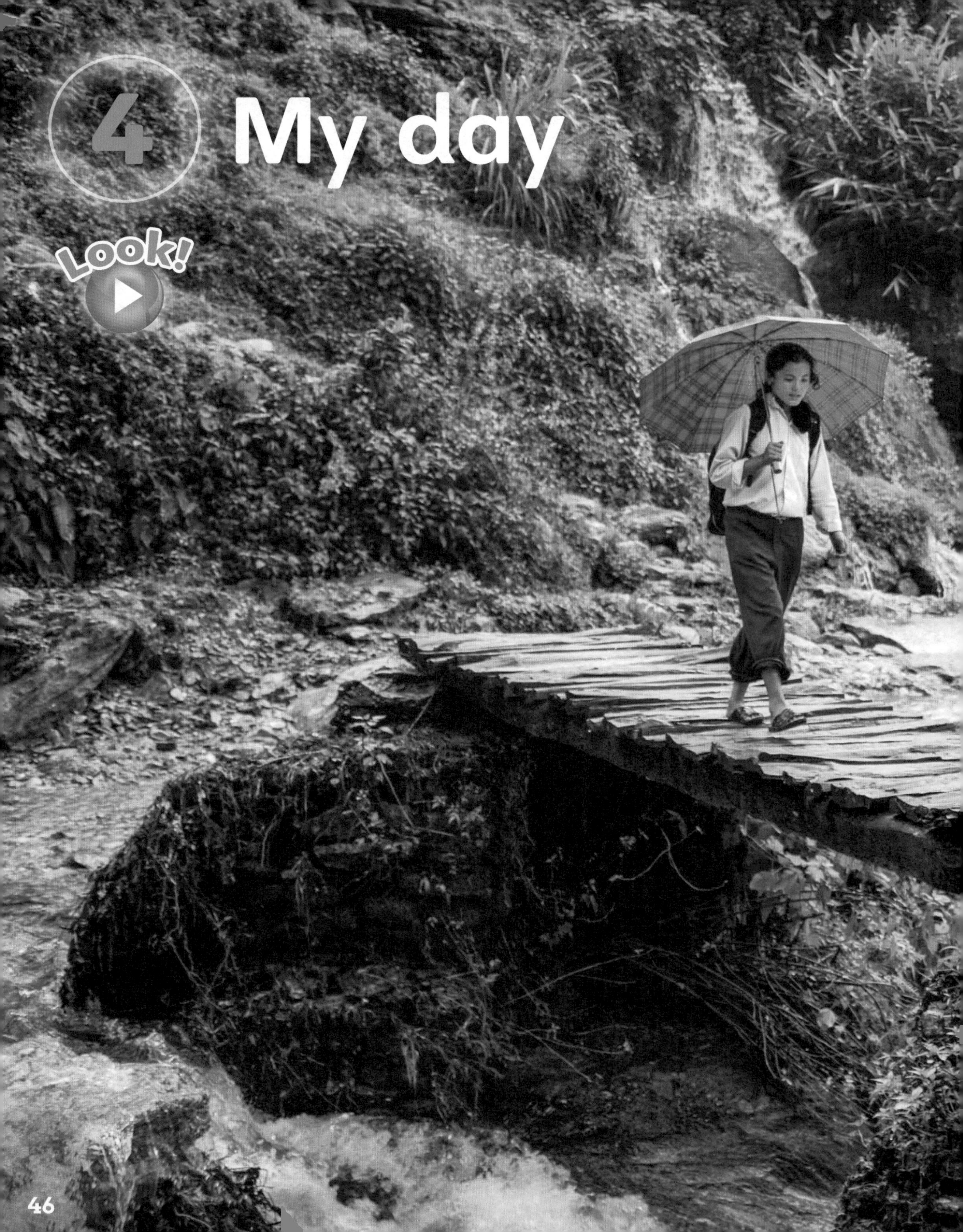

Guess What!

1 4.01 Listen and point.

2 4.02 Listen, point, and repeat.

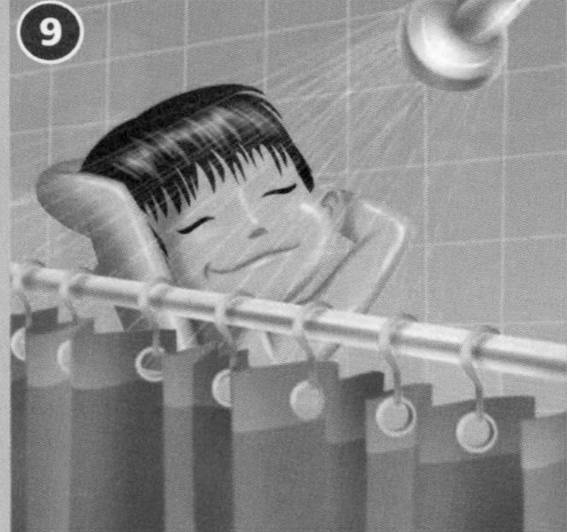

1. get up
2. get dressed
3. have breakfast
4. brush my teeth
5. go to school
6. have lunch
7. go home
8. have dinner
9. take a shower
10. go to bed

3 4.03 Listen and say the numbers.

4  Say the actions and guess the numbers.

Go home. Number 7!

→ Workbook page 38

5 4.04 Sing the song.

I get up at eight o'clock.
I have breakfast at eight thirty.
I go to school at nine o'clock,
And I have lunch at twelve thirty.
Hey, hey, every day.

I go home at three thirty,
And I play with my friends.
I have dinner at seven thirty.
I go to bed at nine o'clock at night.
Hey, hey, every day.

6 4.05 Listen and say the names.

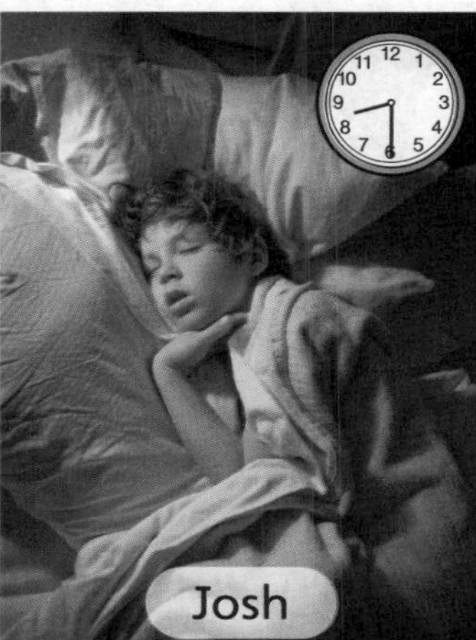

7 About Me Make sentences about your day. Say *true* or *false*.

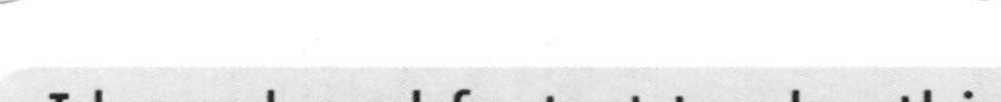

False!

Remember!

I have dinner at seven thirty.
I go to bed at nine o'clock.

Grammar fun!

→ Workbook page 39

8 4.06 Listen and repeat.

9 4.07 About Me Listen and answer.

10 About Me Ask and answer with two friends.

What time do you go to school?

I go to school at nine o'clock.

So do I.

I don't. I go to school at eight thirty.

11 4.08 Go to page 102. Listen and repeat the chant.

Remember

What time do you get up?
I get up at seven o'clock.
So do I. I don't.

→ Workbook page 40

Skills: *Reading and speaking*

Let's start! **Do you have a healthy lifestyle?**

12 4.09 Read and listen. Then answer the questionnaire.

		A	B
1	Do you get up early?	Yes, I do.	No, I don't.
2	Do you have breakfast every day?	Yes, I do.	No, I don't.
3	Do you brush your teeth in the morning and in the evening?	Yes, I do.	No, I don't.
4	Do you walk or ride your bike to school?	Yes, I do.	No, I don't.
5	Do you play outside with your friends?	Yes, I do.	No, I don't.
6	Do you like eating fruits and vegetables?	Yes, I do.	No, I don't.
7	Do you like drinking water or milk?	Yes, I do.	No, I don't.
8	Do you go to bed early?	Yes, I do.	No, I don't.

Mostly As – Good job! You have a healthy lifestyle.
Mostly Bs – Hmm! What can you do to be more healthy?

13 Now ask and answer with a friend.

Do you get up early?

Yes, I do. I get up at seven thirty.

Writing

Workbook page 41: Write your own questionnaire.

14
4.10
Story
Read and listen. Watch.
1
Excuse me. What time is it, please?
It's five o'clock.
Hurry up, Lucas. We're late for swimming club.
2
Find a watch.
3
SWIMMI
SWIMMING RACE TODAY! 5:30 - FIRST PRIZE A WATCH
Look! A swimming race!
The first prize is a watch!
4
I can do the race!
Yes, good idea!
5
Ready, set, go!
Come on, Lucas!
6
And the winner is … Lucas!
Hooray!
7
Good job, Lucas!
Thanks! Swimming is fun!
It's a nice watch!
Value: Exercise
→ Workbook page 42

  Listen and repeat. Then act.

five o'clock   four thirty   nine thirty   eight o'clock

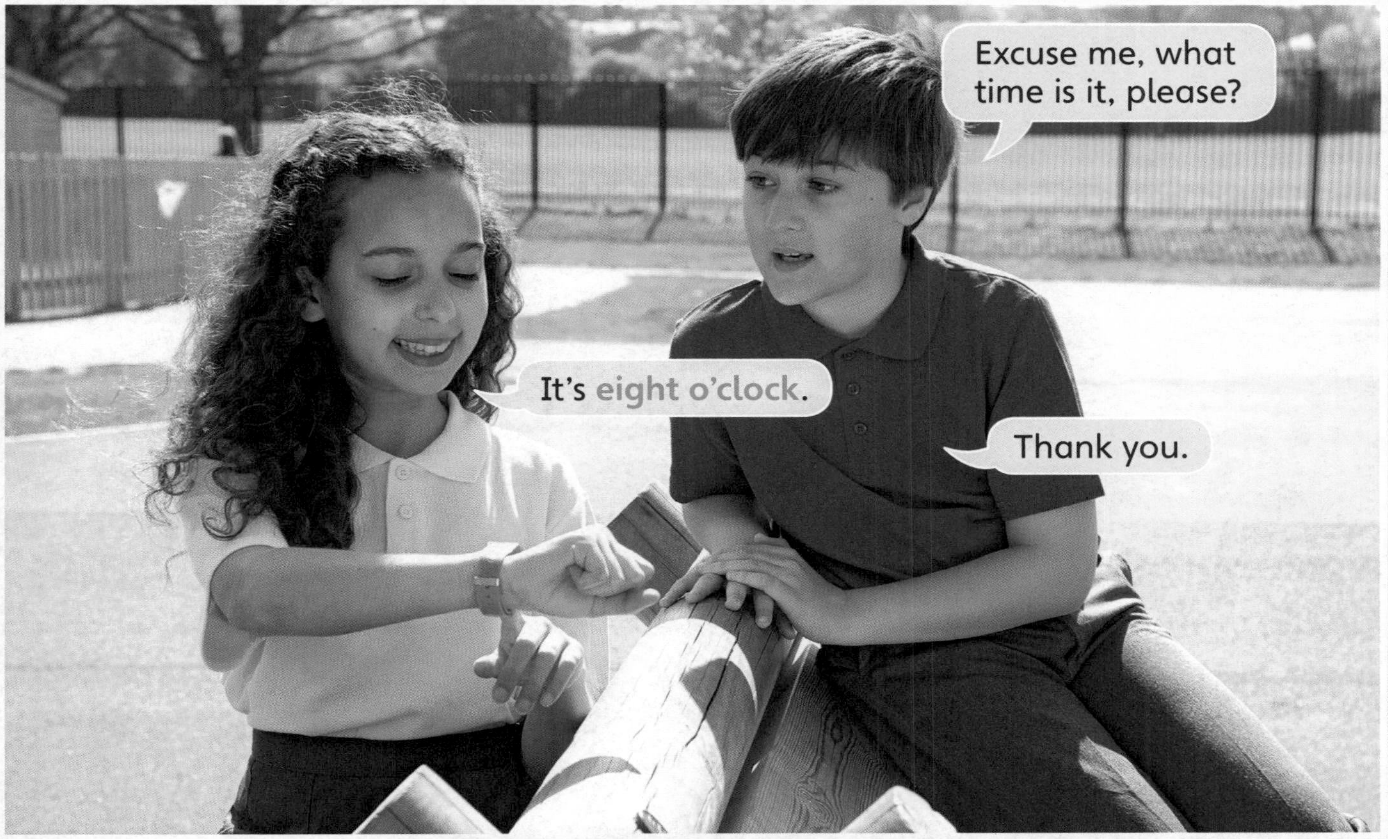

Excuse me, what time is it, please?

It's eight o'clock.

Thank you.

Say it!

16 Listen and repeat.

Blue whales don't chew their food.

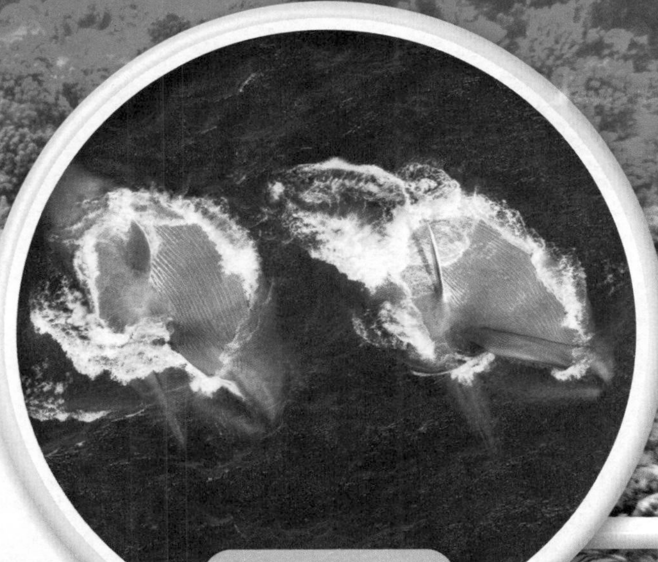

→ Workbook page 43

What time is it around the world?

1 4.13 Listen and repeat.

twelve o'clock

sixteen fifteen

ten thirty

twenty-three forty-five

2 CLIL Watch the video.

3 Match the pictures with the cities on page 54. What time is it?

Let's collaborate!

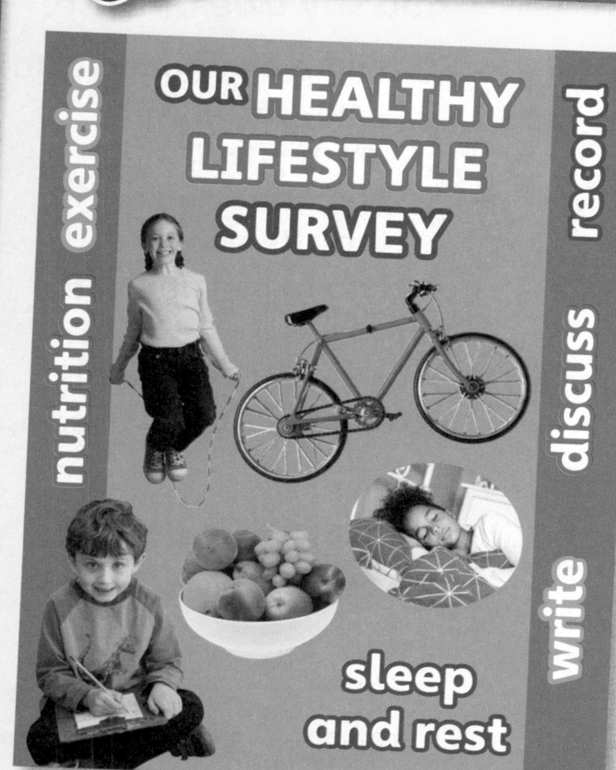

4 What time is it in your country?

→ Workbook page 44

Review

Units 3 and 4

1 **Find the words in the puzzles and match to the photographs.**

g* t* b*d

h*v* br**kf*st

pl*y t*nn*s

g* t* *rt cl*b

2 4.14 **Listen and say the numbers.**

3 **Read Clara's sentences and say *true* or *false*.**

1 I have eggs for breakfast.
2 I play soccer with my friends.
3 I have art club in the afternoon.
4 I go to bed at home.

4 **Make your own word puzzles for your friend.**

Choose days of the week or daily activities:
S*nd*y
T**sd*y

→ Workbook pages 46–47

5 Play the game.

Yellow
What time do you (get up)?
I (get up) at (seven thirty).

Green
What do you have on (Monday) in the (morning)?
I have (English) at (nine o'clock).

5 Home time

Guess What!

1. drink juice
2. eat a sandwich
3. do the dishes
4. play on the computer
5. read a book
6. watch TV
7. do homework
8. listen to music
9. make a cake
10. wash the car

3 (5.03) **Listen and answer the questions.**

1. Is he drinking juice? — Yes, he is.

4 Think **Describe and guess the numbers.**

She's making a cake. — Number 9!

→ Workbook page 48

5 Sing the song.

We are all different,
In my family.
We are all different,
My family and me.

I like listening to music,
But I don't like reading books.
My mom loves reading books,
But she doesn't like watching TV.

My sister enjoys watching TV,
But she doesn't like making cakes.
My dad loves making cakes,
But he doesn't like listening to music.

6 Make sentences about the song and say who.

He enjoys listening to music. Alex!

7 About Me Ask and answer with your friend. Then tell another friend.

Remember!

He **likes** listening to music.
He **doesn't like** reading books.
She **enjoys** watching TV.
She **loves** playing on the computer.

Grammar fun!

8 Look at the photographs and choose. Then listen and repeat.

1

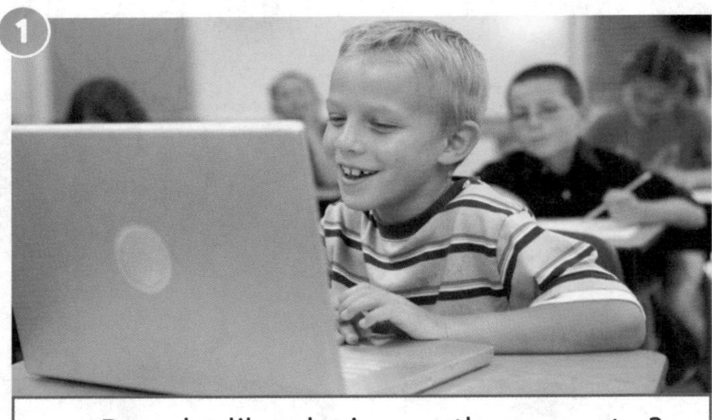

Does he like playing on the computer?
Yes, he does. / No, he doesn't.

2

Does she enjoy washing the car?
Yes, she does. / No, she doesn't.

9 Listen and find. Then answer the question.

10 Ask and answer with a friend.

Does Lina like doing homework?

Yes, she does.

11 Go to page 103. Listen and repeat the chant.

Remember!

Does he **enjoy** doing the dishes?
Yes, he **does**. No, he **doesn't**.

Skills: *Listening and speaking*

Are you helpful at home?

12 5.08 **Listen and choose.**

1 Isabella likes / doesn't like cleaning her bedroom.
2 She enjoys / doesn't enjoy washing the car.
3 She likes / doesn't like doing the dishes.
4 Brad likes / doesn't like cleaning his bedroom.
5 He enjoys / doesn't enjoy washing his bike.
6 He enjoys / doesn't enjoy making cakes.

13  **Ask and answer with a friend.**

Do you like cleaning your bedroom?
Do you like washing the car?
Do you like doing the dishes?
Do you like making cakes?

Writing

➔ Workbook page 51: Write about being helpful at home.

14 5.09 Story Read and listen. Watch.

1
Find a chocolate cake.

2
Let's make the cake.
My aunt Pat likes making cakes.
Great! Let's go to her house!

3
What do we need?
Eggs, milk, chocolate …
OK. Here we are.

4
This is fun!
Oh, dear! Anna loves chocolate cake!
Anna! Stop that!

5
Look! It's great!
Good job!
Let's add some chocolate eggs.

6

7

Value: Show forgiveness
→ Workbook page 52

  **Listen and repeat. Then act.**

chocolate cake cheese sandwich carrot cake
sausage sandwich chicken sandwich

Say it!

16 **Listen and repeat.**

Panthers learn to hunt three months after birth.

Where do people live?

1 Listen and repeat.

countryside

village

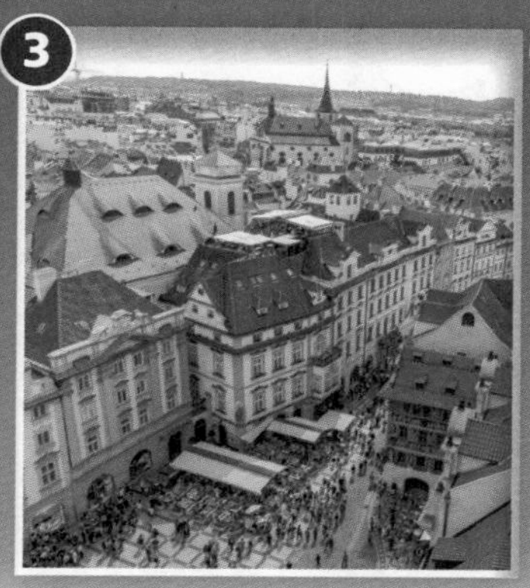
town

city

2 Watch the video.

CLIL

Guess What!
There are more chickens in the world than people.

3 What can you see in the pictures?

4 Where would you like to live?

Let's collaborate!

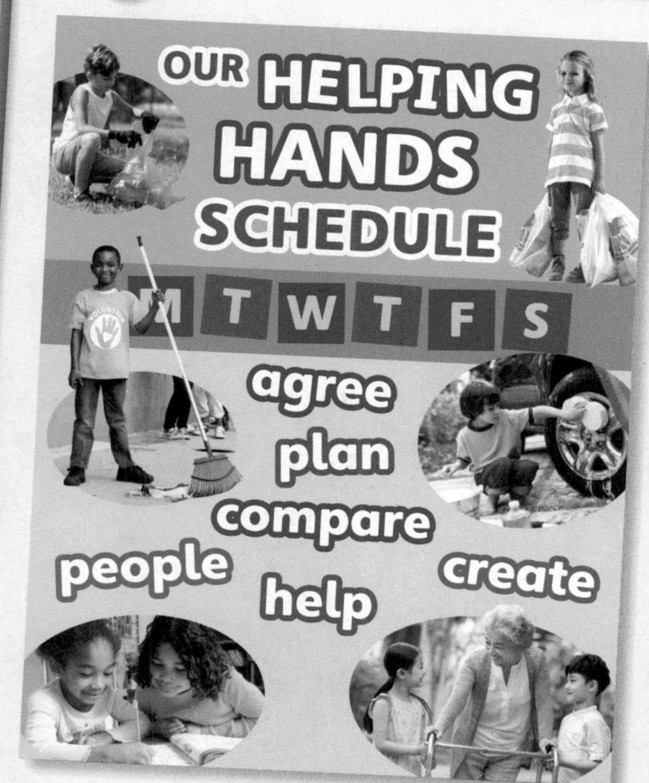

→ Workbook page 54

6 Hobbies

Guess What!

Weekend Clubs and Activities

music clubs

craft clubs

sports clubs

1. play the piano
2. play the guitar
3. play the recorder
4. make models
5. make movies
6. do karate
7. do gymnastics
8. play Ping-Pong
9. play badminton
10. play volleyball

Is he playing the piano?

No, he isn't.

Is he making a model?

Yes, he is.

Number 4!

→ Workbook page 56

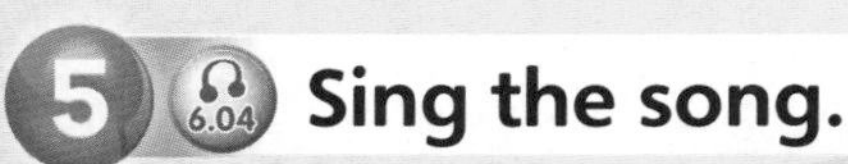

5 Sing the song.

This is our friend Lizzie.
She's very busy!

She plays badminton on Saturdays,
And she does karate on Sundays.
She makes models after school on Wednesdays,
And she makes movies on Mondays.

She doesn't play on the computer,
And she doesn't watch TV after school.
She plays the guitar in the morning,
And she plays the piano in the afternoon.

We like our friend Lizzie.
She's very busy!

6 Make sentences about the song. Say *true* or *false*.

Lizzie doesn't play badminton on Saturdays. False!

7 Ask and answer with your friend. Then tell another friend.

Remember!

She **does** karate on Sundays.
She **doesn't watch** TV after school.
She **plays** the guitar in the morning.

Grammar fun!

8 Look and choose. Then listen and repeat.

1

Jimmy,
Don't forget tennis club on Tuesday.

Does he play tennis on Tuesdays?
Yes, he does. / No, he doesn't.

2

Leah – Remember volleyball club after school.

Does she play volleyball in the morning?
Yes, she does. / No, she doesn't.

9 Listen and answer the questions.

10 Ask and answer about your friends.

Does George do karate after school?

Yes, he does.

11 Go to page 103. Listen and repeat the chant.

Remember

Does she do gymnastics in the evening?
Yes, she **does**. No, she **doesn't**.

Grammar fun!

Skills: *Reading and speaking*

Let's start! **What sports do you like?**

12 Read and listen. Then match.

6.08

Sports we like

Meet Josh. He's ten years old, and he wants to be a soccer player.

Josh goes to a soccer club on Tuesdays and Thursdays after school. He plays soccer on Saturdays and Sundays, too. Josh also plays basketball, and he goes swimming.

Josh has a healthy diet. His favorite dinner is chicken with potatoes or rice and vegetables. He likes fruit, too. His favorite drink is a banana milkshake!

13 Read again and answer the questions.

1 What club does Josh go to?
2 Does he play soccer on Saturdays?
3 Does he play other sports?
4 Does he eat fruits and vegetables?

14 About Me Ask and answer with a friend.

Do you go to a club after school?
What sports do you play?
Do you have a healthy diet?
Which fruits and vegetables do you like?

Writing

Workbook page 59: Write about your favorite sport.

 Value: Try new things

→ Workbook page 60

  Talk Time **Listen and repeat. Then act.**

play the guitar · make models · do gymnastics · do karate · play Ping-Pong

Say it!

17 **Listen and repeat.**

Sharks are fish with sharp teeth.

→ Workbook page 61

What type of musical instrument is it?

1 Listen and repeat.

brass

percussion

string

woodwind

piano

2 CLIL Watch the video.

3 What type of musical instruments can you see?

4 What type of instrument would you like to play?

→ Workbook page 62

Units 5 and 6

1 **Find the words in the puzzles and match to the photographs.**

od scitsanmyg

yalp llabyellov

tae a hciwdnas

netsil ot cisum

2 6.13 **Listen and say the names.**

3 **Read and say the names.**

1 She likes listening to music.
2 He goes to gymnastics club on Tuesdays.
3 She plays volleyball after school.
4 He likes eating sandwiches.

4 **Make your own word puzzles for your friend.**

Choose indoor or outdoor activities:
hsaw eht rac
ekam a ekac

→ Workbook pages 64–65

5 Play the game.

7 At the market

Guess What!

1 7.01 **Listen and point.**

2 7.02 **Listen, point, and repeat.**

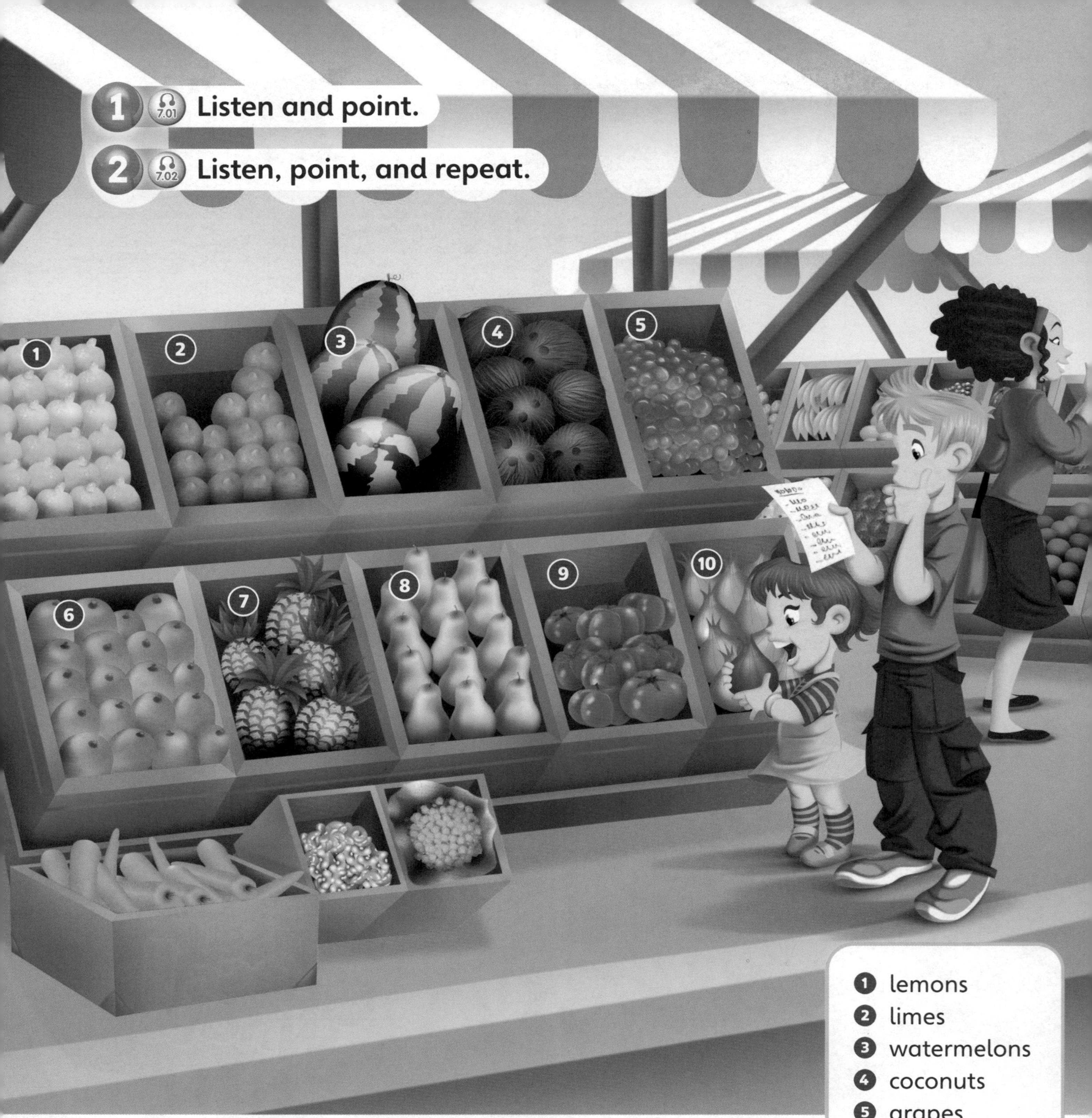

1. lemons
2. limes
3. watermelons
4. coconuts
5. grapes
6. mangoes
7. pineapples
8. pears
9. tomatoes
10. onions

3 7.03 **Listen and say the fruits and vegetables.**

4 Think **Describe and guess what.**

These fruits are small and yellow.

Lemons!

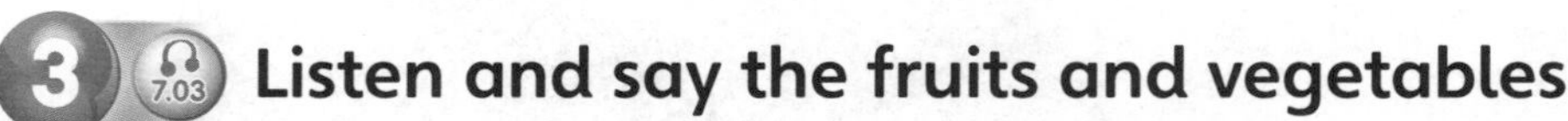

→ Workbook page 66

5 Sing the song.

Come and buy some fruit
At my market stall today!

There are lots of pineapples,
And there are some pears,
But there aren't any mangoes
At your market stall today.

Come and buy some fruit
At my market stall today!

There are lots of lemons,
And there are some limes,
But there aren't any tomatoes
At your market stall today.

6 Look at the song and find the differences in this picture.

There are lots of grapes.

7 Say what you can buy in your town market.

There are lots of lemons in my town market.

Remember!

There are lots of grapes.
There are some tomatoes.
There aren't any limes.

Grammar fun!

8 Listen and repeat.

9 Think Look at the picture. Then cover it and play a memory game.

Are there any mangoes? No, there aren't.

10  Ask and answer about your classroom.

Are there any books? Yes, there are.

Remember

Are there **any** pears?
Yes, there **are**.
No, there **aren't**.

11  Go to page 103. Listen and repeat the chant.

Skills: *Listening and speaking*

Do you like smoothies?

12 Listen and say the numbers.

2 Tropical Mix with ...
Pineapple
Banana
Orange juice

1 Mango Cooler with ...
Banana
Mango
Orange juice

3 Tutti Frutti with ...
Pineapple
Grapes
Watermelon

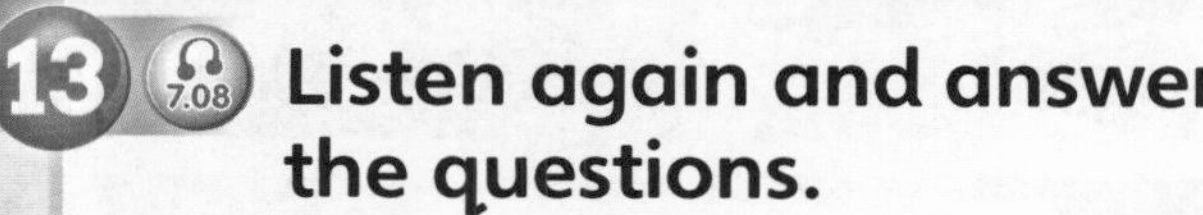

13 Listen again and answer the questions.

1 Does Emilio like bananas?
2 What are Arianna's favorite fruit?
3 Does Marco like orange juice?

14  Ask and answer with a friend.

What is your favorite smoothie?
What is your favorite fruit?
Which smoothie don't you like?
Which fruit don't you like?

Writing

 Workbook page 69: Write about your favorite smoothie.

15 7.09 Story Read and listen. Watch.

Value: Reuse old things

→ Workbook page 70

16 Listen and repeat. Then act.

brown watch **red** purse **blue** guitar **white** radio

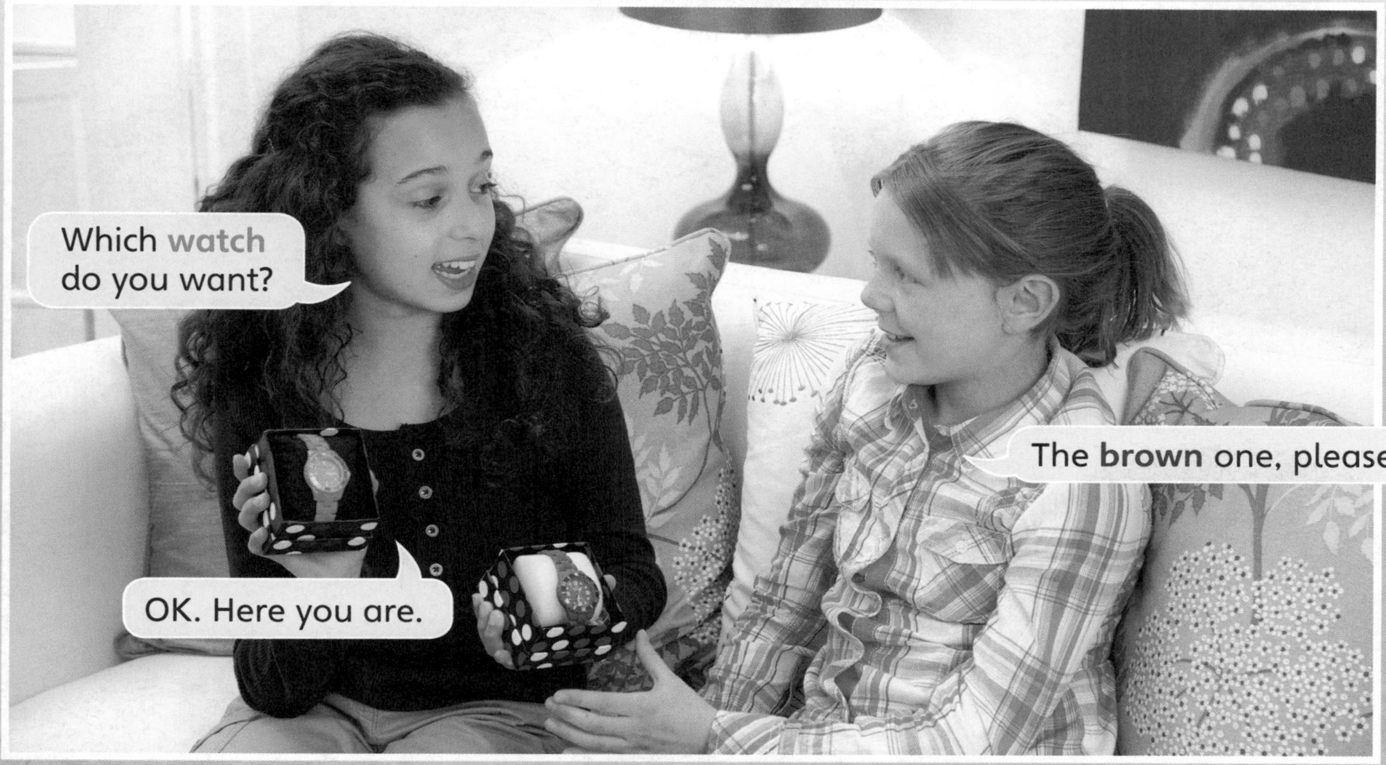

Which watch do you want?

The **brown** one, please.

OK. Here you are.

Say it!

17 Listen and repeat.

Chipmunks have big cheek pouches.

What parts of plants can we eat?

1 Listen and repeat. 7.12

2 CLIL Watch the video.

3 Match the fruits and vegetables with the plant parts.

roots
stems
leaves
fruit
seeds

Guess What!
Some plants eat small frogs and lizards.

Let's collaborate!

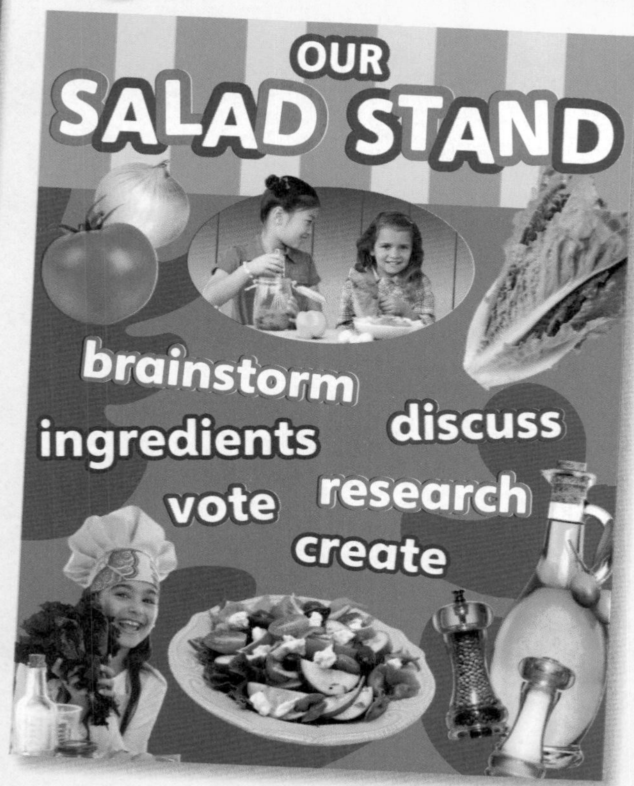

4 What plants do you like to eat?

8 At the beach

Guess What!

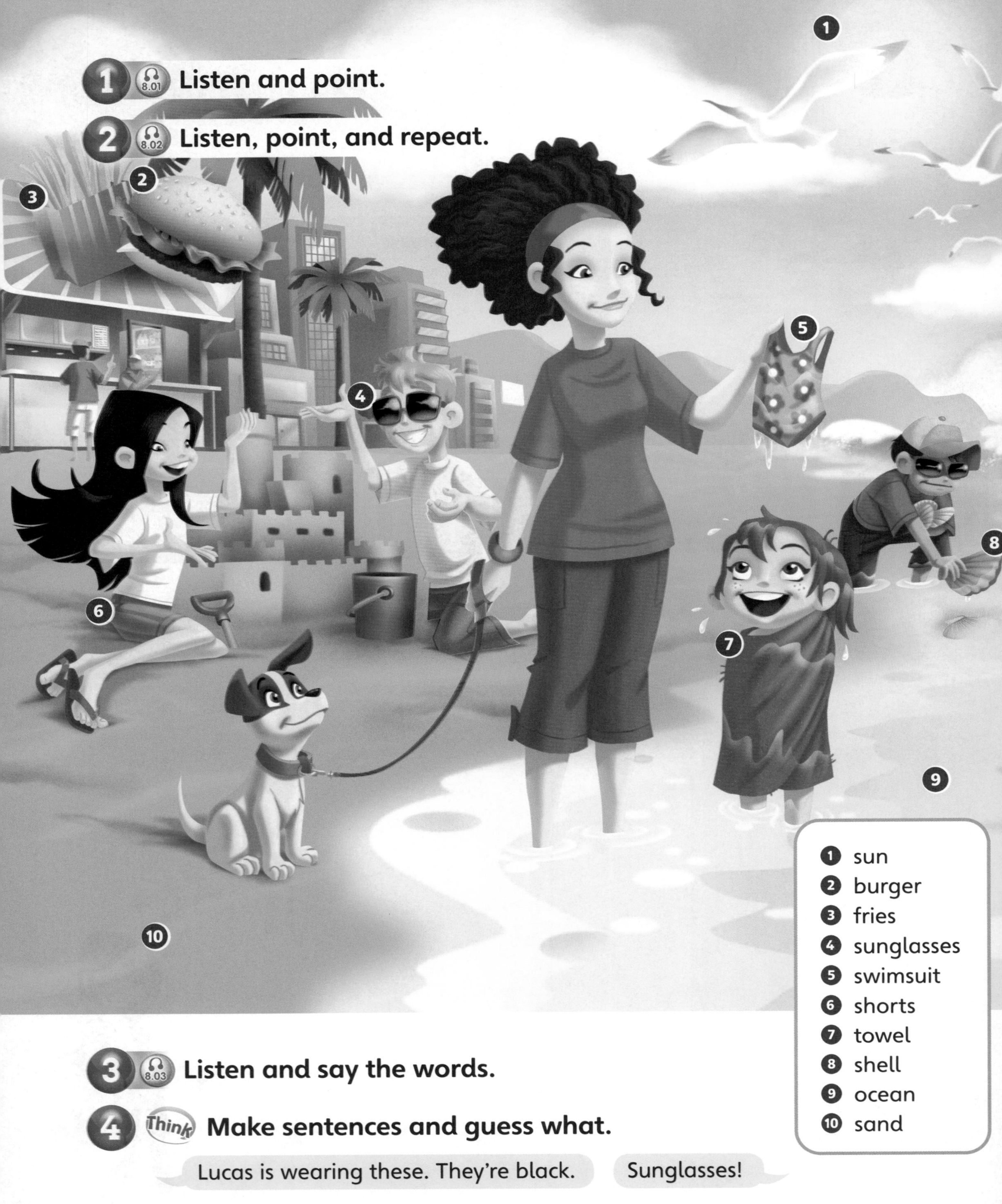

1 8.01 **Listen and point.**

2 8.02 **Listen, point, and repeat.**

1. sun
2. burger
3. fries
4. sunglasses
5. swimsuit
6. shorts
7. towel
8. shell
9. ocean
10. sand

3 8.03 **Listen and say the words.**

4 Think **Make sentences and guess what.**

Lucas is wearing these. They're black.

Sunglasses!

→ Workbook page 74

5 Sing the song.

Which hat is yours?
The red one's mine.
Which hat is yours?
The blue one.

Which sock is hers?
The green one's hers.
Which sock is his?
The yellow one.

Which towel is ours?
The pink one's ours.
Which towel is theirs?
The purple one.

6 Look at the song. Then read and match.

1 Which towel is ours?

2 Which sock is hers?

3 Which hat is yours?

4 Which sock is his?

5 Which towel is theirs?

a The green one's hers.
b The yellow one's his.
c The blue one's mine.
d The purple one.
e The pink one.

7 About Me Ask and answer about your classroom.

Which pencil case is yours?

The purple one's mine.

Remember

Which sock is **hers**?
The green **one's hers**.
Which towel is **theirs**?
The purple **one**.

8 8.05 Listen and repeat.

9 About Me Find these things in your classroom. Then ask and answer.

Whose backpack is this? It's Mark's.

10 8.06 Go to page 103. Listen and repeat the chant.

Remember!

Whose glasses **are these?**
They're mine.

→ Workbook page 76

Skills: *Reading and speaking*

Let's start! What do you like doing on vacation?

11 8.07 Read and listen. Then match.

Dear Grandma and Grandpa,

We're having a great vacation. Can you see the hotel next to the beach? That's ours!

The beach is great. We like playing in the sand. There are lots of shells. We like making pictures with them.

In the evening, we go to the café on the beach. You can see it in this photograph. I like eating burger and fries. They're delicious!

See you soon!

Love from Louis

a

b

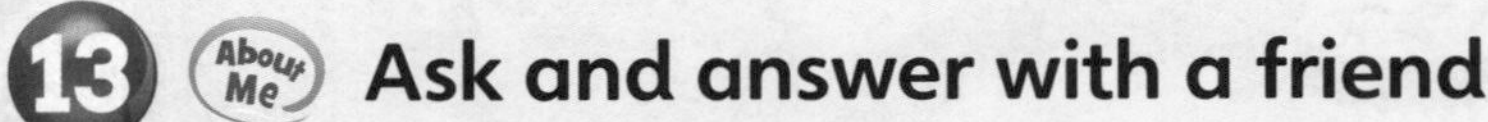

12 Read and say *true* or *false*.

1 Their hotel is next to a forest.
2 They like playing on the beach.
3 There aren't any shells on the beach.
4 Louis likes eating chicken and fries.

13 About Me Ask and answer with a friend.

Where do you like going on vacation?
Who do you go on vacation with?
What do you do on vacation?
What do you like eating on vacation?

Writing

Workbook page 77: Write a postcard to a friend.

Value: Appreciate your family and friends

→ Workbook page 78

  **15** 8.09 Talk Time **Listen and repeat. Then act.**

by plane | by bike | on foot | by train | by car | by bus

Say it!

16 8.10 **Listen and repeat.**

Dolphins are friendly and eat fish.

→ Workbook page 79

Are sea animals symmetrical?

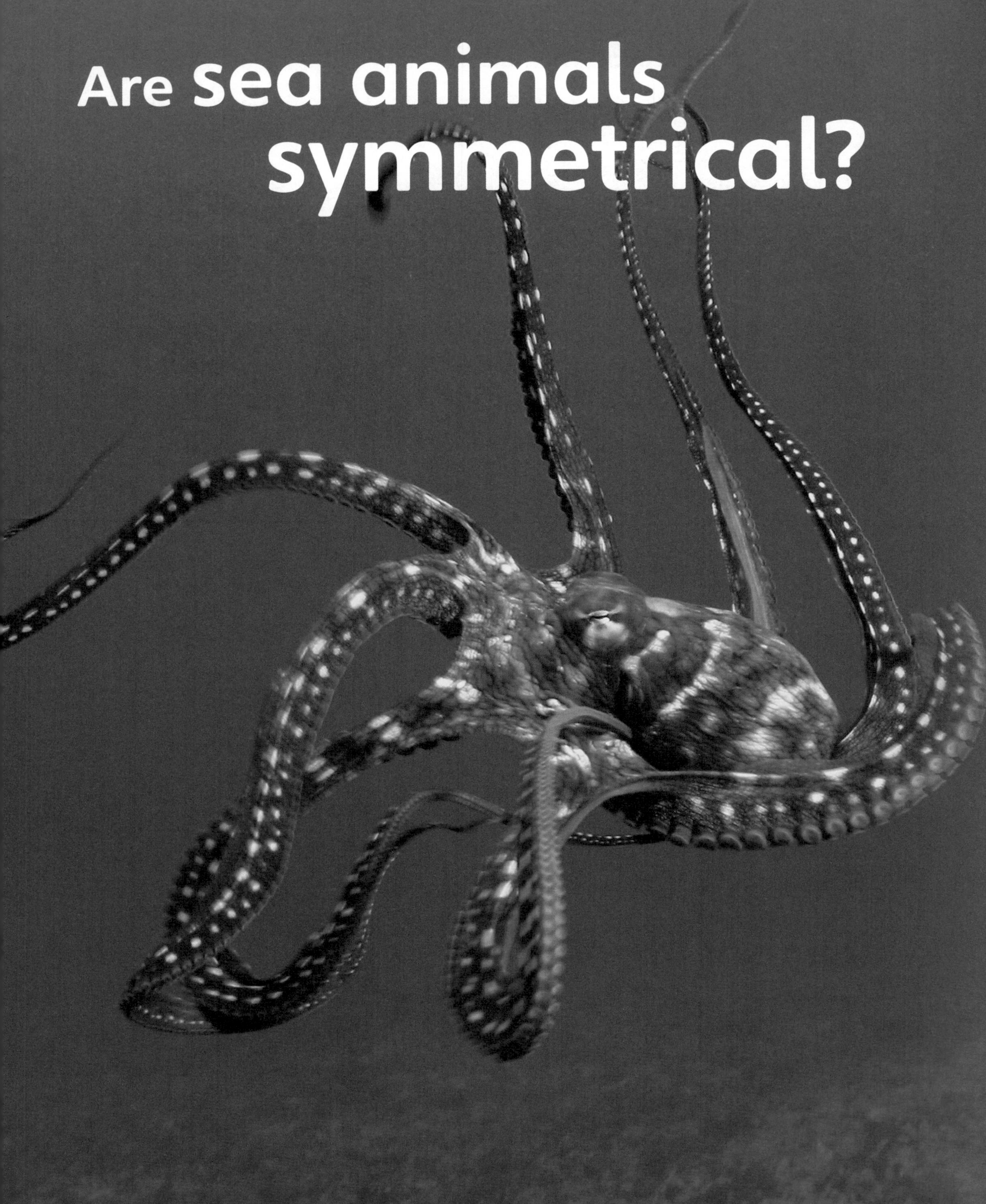

1 8.11 Listen and repeat.

1 starfish | 2 crab | 3 jellyfish | 4 octopus | 5 sea horse

2 CLIL Watch the video.

3 In these pictures, which sea animals are symmetrical?

1

2

3

4
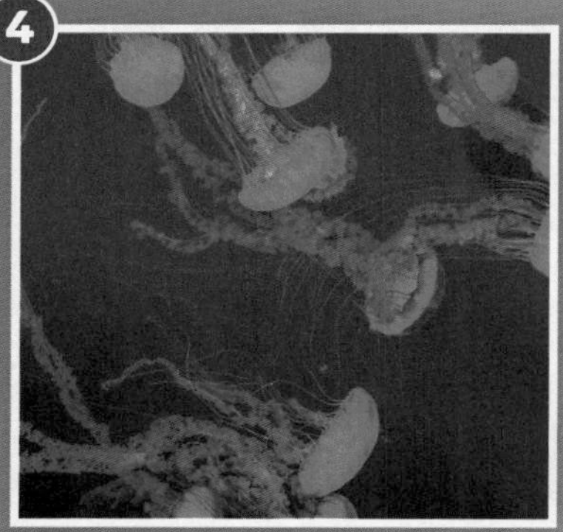

Let's collaborate!

4 Which sea animals do you like?

Review

Units 7 and 8

1 **Find the words and match to the photographs.**

mangoesshellsoceansunglasses

2 8.12 **Listen and say the numbers.**

3 **Answer the questions.**

1 Where are Aiden and his sister playing?
2 Whose shells are on the beach?
3 Are there any mangoes on the beach?
4 Are there any sunglasses at the market?

4 **Make your own word puzzles for your friend.**

Choose fruits or vegetables:
lemonslimespears

→ Workbook pages 82–83

5 Play the game.

Start

Is there a gym in Lucas's school? (See Unit 2)

Whose painting is this?

Are there any apples at the market? (See Unit 7)

Whose presents are these?

Are there any animals in Lucas's yard? (See Unit 1)

Whose tiger is this?

#1

Whose dog is this?

Are there any shells at the beach? (See Unit 8)

Whose sunglasses are these?

Are there any butterflies in the park? (See Unit 1)

Whose aunt is this?

Is there a computer at Tom's house? (See Unit 5)

Start

Chants

Welcome (page 8)

Listen and repeat the chant.

When's your birthday?
It's in June.
January, February, and March,
April, May, and June.

When's your birthday?
It's in December.
July, August, and September,
October, November, and December.

Unit 1 (page 18)

Listen and repeat the chant.

What's that?
It's a snail.
What are those?
They're butterflies.

What's that?
It's a snake.
What are those?
They're leaves.

Unit 2 (page 28)

Listen and repeat the chant.

What are you doing?
We're playing tennis.
What are they doing?
They're playing tennis.

What are you doing?
We're playing baseball.
What are they doing?
They're playing baseball.

Unit 3 (page 40)

Listen and repeat the chant.

What class does she have after lunch?
She has art after lunch.
What class does she have after lunch?
She has art.

What club does she have after school?
She has swimming club after school.
What club does she have after school?
She has swimming club.

Unit 4 (page 50)

Listen and repeat the chant.

What time do you have breakfast?
I have breakfast at eight o'clock.
So do I.
I don't.
I have breakfast at seven thirty.

What time do you go to school?
I go to school at nine o'clock.
So do I.
I don't.
I go to school at eight thirty.

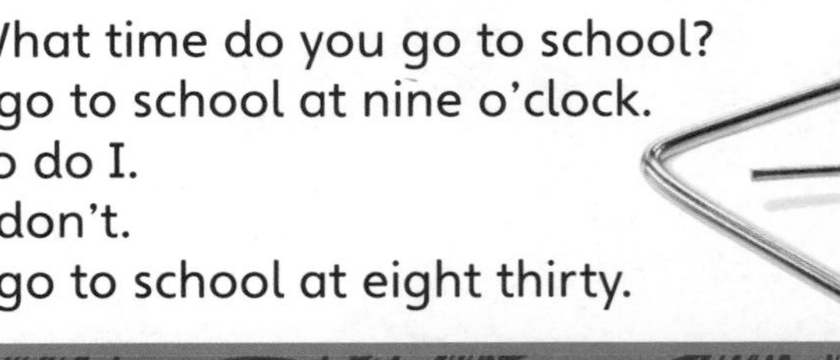

Unit 5 (page 62)

Listen and repeat the chant.

Does he like playing on the computer?
Yes, he does. Yes, he does.
Does she enjoy washing the car?
No, she doesn't. No, she doesn't.

Does she like doing homework?
Yes, she does. Yes, she does.
Does he enjoy reading books?
No, he doesn't. No, he doesn't.

Unit 6 (page 72)

Listen and repeat the chant.

Does he play tennis on Tuesdays?
Yes, he does. Yes, he does.
Does she play volleyball in the morning?
No, she doesn't. No, she doesn't.

Does he do karate after school?
Yes, he does. Yes, he does.
Does she do gymnastics in the evening?
No, she doesn't. No, she doesn't.

Unit 7 (page 84)

Listen and repeat the chant.

Are there any onions?
Yes, there are. Yes, there are.
Are there any coconuts?
No, there aren't. No, there aren't.

Are there any pears?
Yes, there are. Yes, there are.
Are there any mangoes?
No, there aren't. No, there aren't.

Unit 8 (page 94)

Listen and repeat the chant.

Whose jacket is this?
It's mine. It's mine.
Whose shoes are these?
They're Sally's.

Whose backpack is this?
It's Mark's. It's Mark's.
Whose glasses are these?
They're mine.

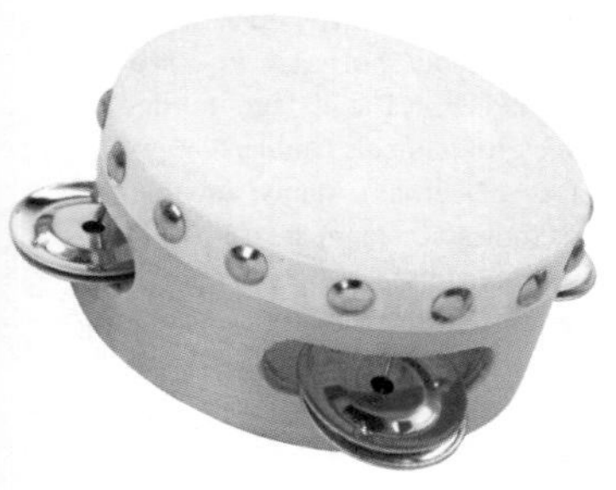

Acknowledgments

Many thanks to everyone in the excellent team at Cambridge University Press & Assessment in Spain, the UK, and India.

The authors and publishers would like to thank the following contributors:
Blooberry Design: concept design, cover design, book design
Hyphen: publishing management, page make-up
Ann Thomson: art direction
Gareth Boden: commissioned photography
Jon Barlow: commissioned photography
Ian Harker: class audio recording
John Marshall Media: "Grammar fun" recordings
Robert Lee, Dib Dib Dub Studios: song and chant composition
Vince Cross: theme tune composition
James Richardson: arrangement of theme tune
Phaebus: "CLIL" video production
Kiki Foster: "Look!" video production
Bill Smith Group: "Grammar fun" and story animations
Sounds Like Mike Ltd: "Grammar Fun" video production

The authors and publishers acknowledge the following sources of copyright material and are grateful for the permissions granted. While every effort has been made, it has not always been possible to identify the sources of all the material used, or to trace all copyright holders. If any omissions are brought to our notice, we will be happy to include the appropriate acknowledgements on reprinting and in the next update to the digital edition, as applicable.

Key: U = Unit.

Photography

The following photos are sourced from Getty Images:
U0: kali9/E+; zianlob/iStock/Getty Images Plus; Martin Harvey/The Image Bank; jaroon/E+; IndiaPix/IndiaPicture; Jose Luis Pelaez Inc/DigitalVision; XiXinXing; damircudic/E+; **U1:** Tatiana Lobanova/iStock/Getty Images Plus; szefei/iStock/Getty Images Plus; Cavan Images; ivanmateev/iStock/Getty Images Plus; Darrell Gulin/The Image Bank; Antagain/E+; arlindo71/E+; a.collectionRF/amana images; Prasit photo/Moment; MILATAS; Corey Hochachka/Design Pics; **U2:** MichaelDeLeon/E+; MNStudio/iStock/Getty Images Plus; Pablo Alberto Velasco Ibarra/EyeEM; Janie Airey/DigitalVision; Jupiterimages/Stockbyte; Brand X Pictures/Stockbyte; Sergiy Trofimov Photography/Moment; Mint Images/Mint Images; Huber\u0026 Starke/Corbis; globestock/E+; Andersen Ross Photography Inc/DigitalVision; Klaus Vedfelt/DigitalVision; **U3:** Bartosz Hadyniak/E+; Daniel R Monroe/500px; Mike Kemp/Tetra images; Lane Oatey/Blue Jean Images/blue jean images; WIN-Initiative/Neleman/Stone; The Good Brigade/DigitalVision; MichaelDeLeon/E+; **U4:** Stephen Simpson/Stone; Juanmonino/E+; nehopelon/iStock/Getty Images Plus; Barry Downard; Shy Al Britanni/arabianEye; Rosemary Calvert/Photographer's Choice; Photodisc; THEPALMER/E+; Milko/E+; Marc Romanelli/Tetra images; **U5:** Marc Debnam/Photodisc; Ryan McVay/Photodisc; Pablo Alberto Velasco Ibarra/EyeEM; slowmotiongli/iStock/Getty Images Plus; lucky-photographer/iStock Editorial; Mimadeo/iStock/Getty Images Plus; Subodh Agnihotri/iStock/Getty Images Plus; Goads Agency/E+; Lane Oatey/Blue Jean Images/blue jean images; Dev Carr/Image Source; Kraig Scarbinsky/DigitalVision; Wealan Pollard/OJO Images; Hill Street Studios/DigitalVision; **U6:** TadejZupancic/E+; monkeybusinessimages/iStock/Getty Images Plus; Jose Luis Pelaez Inc/DigitalVision; Erik Isakson/Tetra images; Barry Downard; Hugh Sitton/Stone; Gary S Chapman/Photographer's Choice; Mr_Twister/iStock/Getty Images Plus; Salvator Barki/Moment; Nick Rowe/Stockbyte; Scott Van Dyke/Corbis Documentary;SEAN GLADWELL/Moment; PhotoAlto Agency Collections; Dhemmy Zeirifandi; mbbirdy/E+; mladn61/E+; Wattanaphob Kappago; Westend61; Terry Vine/DigitalVision; PhotoAlto/PhotoAlto Agency Collections; **U7:** rudi_suardi/iStock Unreleased; Kingfisher Productions/DigitalVision; George Contorakes; szefei/iStock/Getty Images Plus; Phillip Hayson/Stockbyte; mbbirdy/E+; Richard Clark/The Image Bank; dogayusufdokdok/E+; Creativeye99/E+; MW/Stockbyte; ruizluquepaz/E+; Mike Kemp/Tetra images; **U8:** A bflo photo/Moment Open; Barry Downard; Stuart Westmorland/Corbis Documentary; Medioimages/Photodisc; SolStock/E+; Jose Luis Pelaez Inc/DigitalVision; Elisabeth Schmitt/Moment; JulPo/E+; Floortje/E+; FatCamera/E+; RedHelga/iStock/Getty Images Plus.

The following photos are sourced from other libraries:
U0: serhi000111/Shutterstock; TongRo Images/Alamy; KPG-Payless/Shutterstock; Robert Daly/OJO Images Ltd/Alamy; Robert Harding World Imagery/Alamy; Martyn Goddard/Alamy; Jaroslaw Grudzinski/Shutterstock; Galyna Andrushko/Shutterstock; Nicha/Shutterstock; konzeptm/Shutterstock; Calin Tatu/Shutterstock; iBird/Shutterstock; nodff/Shutterstock; antpkr/Shutterstock; Lillya Kulianionak/Shutterstock; **U1:** crazychris84/Shutterstock; Sergii Figurnyi/Shutterstock; ARTSILENSE/Shutterstock; Ivan Cholakov/Shutterstock; nrey/Shutterstock; Michael Warwick/Shutterstock; Matt Jeppson/Shutterstock; carlos Villoch-MagicSea.com/Alamy; jajaladdawan/Shutterstock; FloridaStock/Shutterstock; Ernie Janes/Alamy; retiles4all/Shutterstock; liubomirt/Shutterstock; Ryan M. Bolton/Shutterstock; James Urbach/Purestock/SuperStock/Alamy; James Laurie/Shutterstock; Toshe Ognjanov/Shutterstock; Monkey Business Images/Shutterstock; Liudmila P. Sundikova/Shutterstock; Brocreative/Shutterstock; Laszlo Halasi/Shutterstock; FLPA/Alamy; Luciano Candisani/Minden Pictures/Alamy; Carole-Anne Fooks/Alamy; **U2:** Kike Calvo/National Geographic Society/Corbis; Mark Herreid/Shutterstock; Gabe Palmer/Alamy; Antenna/fStop Images GmbH/Alamy; Tanja Giessler/fStop Images GmbH/Alamy; Lightspring/Shutterstock; Marquisphoto/Shutterstock; Ulrich Mueller/Shutterstock; italianestro/Shutterstock; pixinoo/Shutterstock; Phovoir/Shutterstock; criben/Shutterstock; Sally and Richard Greenhill/Alamy; Peter Bennett/Citizen of the Planet/Alamy; JLP/Jose L. Pelaez/Corbis; **U3:** Trevor Smith/Alamy; IE360/Cultura Creative/Alamy; Christine Langer-Pueschel/Shutterstock; igor kisselev/Shutterstock; Air Images/Shutterstock; Julian Abrams-VIEW/Alamy; ThomasLENNE/Shutterstock; Monkey Business Images/Shutterstock; sianc/Shutterstock; PT Images/Shutterstock; D.Hurst/Alamy; Robert Harding World Imagery/Alamy; Douglas Noblet/All Canada Photos/Alamy; Julian W/Shutterstock; Sandy Hedgepeth/Shutterstock; jakit17/Shutterstock; Dennis W Donohue/Shutterstock; DnDavis/Shutterstock; Moodboard Stock Photography/Alamy; Kim Taylor/Nature Picture Library/Alamy; Theerapol Pongkangsananan/Shutterstock; Ziggylives/Shutterstock; Roman Malanchuk/Shutterstock; rdonar/Shutterstock; **U4:** Kristian Buus/Alamy; Peter Titsmuss/Alamy; Judith Collins/Alamy; Peter Titmus/Alamy; Jill Chen/Shutterstock; Zoonar GmbH/Alamy; Shailth/Shutterstock; Flip Nicklin/Minden Pictures/Alamy; DYLAN MARTINEZ/Reuters/Corbis; Finnbarr Webster/Alamy; Andrew Wood/Alamy; Steve Heap/Shutterstock; Tetra Images/Alamy; Cultura Creative/Alamy; Red Images, LLC/Alamy; Sabina Jane Blackbird/Alamy; Nuchylee/Shutterstock; Monkey Business Images/Shutterstock; chonrawit boonprakob/Shutterstock; **U5:** Adrian Cook/Alamy; D. Hurst/Alamy; Jim West/Alamy; LanKS/Shutterstock; James Osmond/Alamy; Christopher Hill/scenicireland.com/Alamy; Russ Munn/Design Pics Inc/Alamy; incamerastock/Alamy; Scenics & Science/Alamy; Ingvar Bjork/Alamy; **U6:** Inti St Clair/Tetra Images, LLC/Alamy; Zhelunovych/Shutterstock; AiVectors/Shutterstock; nattanan726/Shutterstock; Denis Scott/Corbis; exopixel/Shutterstock; the palms/Shutterstock; Kitch Bain/Shutterstock; Discovod/Shutterstock; Ansis Klucis/Shutterstock; Smileus/Shutterstock; Denys Kurylow/Shutterstock; Tom Pavlasek/Shutterstock; Sergio Schnitzler/Shutterstock; Tetra Images/Alamy; muzsy/Shutterstock; Radius Images/Design Pics/Alamy; **U7:** Valeri Luzina/Shutterstock; Linda Freshwaters Arndt/Alamy; MIXA/SOURCENEXT/Alamy; B. BOISSONNET/BSIP SA/Alamy; Filipe B. Varela/Shutterstock; Sergii Figurnyi/Shutterstock; JIANG HONGYAN/Shutterstock; Yasonya/Shutterstock; Richard Grifffin/Shutterstock; vnlit/Shutterstock; Africa Studio/Shutterstock; Crepesoles/Shutterstock; photosync/Shutterstock; Dulce Rubia/Shutterstock; Preto Perola/Shutterstock; **U8:** LOOK Die Bildagentur der Fotografen GmbH/Alamy; Juergen Richter/Image Professionals GmbH/Alamy; silvae/Shutterstock; WaterFrame_fba/Alamy; David Fleetham/Alamy; aquapix/Shutterstock; sunsinger/Shutterstock; L. Powell/Shutterstock; melissaf84/Shutterstock; Keith Tarrier/Shutterstock; Damsea/Shutterstock; Sergii Figurnyi/Shutterstock; Henry Beeker/Alamy; Ivonne Wierink/Shutterstock; Terry Mathews/Alamy; Elena Schweitzer/Shutterstock.

Front Cover Photography by Olena Kuzina/iStock/Getty Images Plus.

Illustrations

Aphik; A Corazon Abierto; Luke Newell; Marcus Cutler; Mark Duffin; Pablo Gallego.